Outstanding Differentiation for Learning in the Classroom

One of the key features of an outstanding lesson is that all learners make progress. All learners are different and teachers must differentiate according to the individual pupil and their individual learning needs to achieve outstanding progress. *Outstanding Differentiation for Learning in the Classroom* is written with the class teacher in mind and demonstrates how differentiation can be used to enhance and support all aspects of the learning process.

Including chapters on embedding differentiation during each phase of the lesson, on assessment and on questioning techniques, this book will help you to use differentiation effectively to produce outstanding results. With a strong focus on practical strategies to help you meaningfully apply differentiation in the classroom, this book covers:

- what differentiation actually means and why it should be applied in the classroom;
- sequencing and planning for learning with an overview of the learning cycle;
- practical teaching strategies and effective techniques to use in the classroom;
- how to structure and apply differentiation practices in your classroom, department and school.

A vital starting point and effective guide for outstanding differentiation, this timely new book is packed full of practical exercises that are easy to implement in the classroom and it is essential reading for newly qualified and experienced teachers alike.

Dr Jayne Bartlett has worked in education for over ten years in a range of schools with roles at senior leadership level and is currently working freelance as an independent teaching and learning trainer and consultant.

Outstanding Differentiation for Learning in the Classroom

Dr Jayne Bartlett

Routledge
Taylor & Francis Group

LONDON AND NEW YORK

First published 2016
by Routledge
2 Park Square, Milton Park, Abingdon, Oxon OX14 4RN

and by Routledge
711 Third Avenue, New York, NY 10017

Routledge is an imprint of the Taylor & Francis Group, an informa business

British Library Cataloguing in Publication Data
A catalogue record for this book is available from the British Library

Library of Congress Cataloging in Publication Data
A Catalog record for this book has been requested

ISBN: 978-1-138-83904-5 (hbk)
ISBN: 978-1-138-83905-2 (pbk)
ISBN: 978-1-315-73365-4 (ebk)

Typeset in Bembo
by Cenveo Publisher Services

To my wonderful family:

Mum, Dad, David, Darren, Oliver and Olivia

Contents

List of figures and tables

List of figures

x

List of tables

Acknowledgements

I would like to thank Shutterstock for the use of images.

I would also very much like to thank the team at Routledge who have given me this wonderful opportunity (once again!) and who have supported me in developing and creating this book. They are a fantastic team and I can't thank them enough.

Most of all I must thank my family. First my parents, Pauline and George, who as always have provided incredible support and helped tremendously by looking after Oliver and Olivia while I was writing this book, and also my brother David. I thank my husband Darren who has provided great encouragement and endless cups of tea, and Oliver and Olivia who have been really patient while mummy was writing. I have been fortunate to have such wonderful support around me and I thank you all. I dedicate this book to my wonderful family and most importantly to my two amazing children Oliver and Olivia. I am so very proud of them both.

I have thoroughly enjoyed writing this book and I hope that you enjoy reading it. Mostly I hope you employ some of the strategies to help you on your journey to implementing outstanding differentiation in learning.

Introduction

There is a strong emphasis on progress in learning and a key feature of an outstanding lesson is that 'all pupils make progress'. All learners are different. They may have different abilities, different learning styles and different life or learning experiences. If teachers are to ensure that all pupils make progress (albeit at potentially differing rates) then they must differentiate according to the individual pupil and their individual learning needs. When pupils can access learning we begin to see outstanding progress. The strategies we employ are important but we must always be realistic and conscious of a teacher's workload. Differentiation strategies need to support both the process of teaching and the process of learning, creating an environment where all pupils achieve success.

This book is written with the class teacher in mind and different strategies are explored with examples from a range of subjects. The aim is that these are easy to translate to your own subject specialism, enhancing the learning experience in your classroom. As you read this book always keep in mind that there is no 'one size fits all' approach to outstanding and that there is no one style that a teacher must adopt. Outstanding teaching can occur in a classroom where the teacher is conservative in their approach and can equally occur in the classroom where the teacher is 'all singing, all dancing'. Pupil progress underpins outstanding teaching and outstanding learning. This is where we must focus our attention – how to develop *learning* in our classroom – putting pupils at the heart of our planning. Only then will we begin to personalise learning. Differentiation combined with other pedagogies supports this process.

In Chapter 1 we look at the need for differentiation in learning and discuss different aspects of differentiation. We focus on the factors that we may need to consider as we plan for learning and the different types of differentiation strategies that are commonly used in our classrooms. The most recent OFSTED criteria are highlighted and the importance of expectations in the context of learning in the classroom is discussed.

In Chapter 2 we focus on the learning cycle. This has four stages: developing the concept, activating learning, embedding learning and reflection. While it does not matter where we start on the learning cycle, it is important to complete all four stages to secure optimum learning. Activities may be differentiated within a learning cycle as a whole, within different phases or through the use of parallel learning cycles (for example, one learning cycle for the more able but two or more parallel learning cycles for the less able). It is how we sequence learning in a lesson to secure progress that is important. This is discussed in the context of the start of the lesson, main body of the lesson and the plenary. While I do not advocate an explicit three-part structure, I do refer to it throughout this book as most teachers can relate this to their daily practice and then translate the ideas to their own classroom. The focus is on the learning cycles within these phases and how they connect and progress learning through differentiation. It is how we sequence learning that is important.

Chapter 3 is dedicated to the start of the lesson – the learning hook. We discuss the need for bell work when pupils arrive over a short period and the importance of a Big Question to support the assessment of progress. The starter activity does not have to be differentiated and often when we benchmark learning this is the case. At other times we do need to differentiate and both situations are discussed in this chapter. The key is that the starter activity is accessible to all pupils, so that we engage them in learning from the moment they enter the classroom. Otherwise there is the potential for pupils to become disengaged and for low level disruptive behaviour to creep in. Lots of different starter activities are discussed – and their pros and cons - contextualised with material from different subjects. How to structure the start of your lesson is implicit throughout this chapter.

In Chapter 4 we progress to the main body of the lesson. This is not to say that it is a discrete unit but one where we use assessment data from the start of the lesson as a platform for learning. In this section we typically develop concepts and embed learning through a series of mini-assessments. The information we obtain from this process informs our differentiated pathways, usually leading to a longer activity. In this chapter we focus on the different types of activities that are used in the main body of the lesson and the strategies for differentiation; when, how and why we might choose to use them. We discuss different learning styles and how we can use our knowledge of these to design different activities that allow all pupils to access learning. There is emphasis on how we assign pupils to a given pathway and the importance of involving pupils in this choice.

Chapter 5 focuses on the plenary. Typically during this phase of the lesson more emphasis is placed on the reflective process in the learning cycle. It is important that we continue to challenge learning in the plenary and we go beyond simply asking pupils to quote 'what they have learnt today'. We discuss lots of different types of plenary activity (some activities lend themselves better to the plenary than others) and how and if we may need to differentiate them. Lots of different examples are used, which make it easy for you to draw on these techniques in your own practice. We look at how to develop the lesson in order to ensure that progress towards the learning outcome has been measured (qualitatively or quantitatively).

In Chapter 6 we focus on assessment for learning. There is an implicit link between assessment and differentiation. Assessment informs differentiation and differentiated pathways inform assessment. Without assessing learning and knowing exactly where pupils 'are' in their learning then it is difficult to differentiate to ensure maximum progress. The quality of our differentiation is underpinned by the quality of the assessment data. Therefore it is important that formative assessment is used to best effect. In this chapter we review the important role of assessment for learning in differentiation, focusing on different assessment techniques and then looking at how they support any differentiation strategies we may use. We also look closely at different marking and feedback techniques and how they inform best practice.

In Chapter 7 we review different questioning strategies. Questioning is one of the most powerful techniques available to us in the classroom and yet it is so often underused. In this chapter we focus on how to differentiate using questioning and how to develop higher-order thinking skills in all pupils. One of the problems we encounter in the classroom is that teachers will ask lower-order questions to low ability pupils and higher-order questions to the more able. Why? Simply because many teachers seek the correct answer when they ask questions and so they direct them to a learner that they are confident is the most likely to answer correctly (this is particularly true in an observed lesson – cynical I know!). It is essential that we develop higher-order thinking in all pupils and we draw upon Bloom's Taxonomy to support this process, using examples across a range of subjects. We also discuss other factors relating to questioning such as wait time (processing and response) and hands down and how you might move forwards in improving questioning in your classroom.

In Chapter 8 we focus on how to develop differentiation strategies at a department- or whole-school level and how to embed differentiation. Misconceptions within the practice of differentiation are discussed and examples of best and poor practice are compared. We focus on trying to ensure that the impact on teacher workload is minimised while maximising the impact on pupil progress. High quality training is needed to provide teachers with the necessary tools. By providing simple techniques that mean teachers can implement differentiation without adding substantially to their workload – making it an implicit part of planning and learning rather than a discrete tag on – we will impact directly on learning.

In summary, Chapters 1 and 2 introduce you to differentiation and the learning cycle respectively, Chapters 3, 4 and 5 focus specifically on differentiation in different phases of the lesson, Chapters 6 and 7 focus on specific techniques and Chapter 8 focuses on how to embed best practice. I very much hope that you enjoy reading this book and gain lots of ideas to support you on your way to implementing outstanding differentiation strategies in your classroom, leading to all pupils making outstanding progress.

CHAPTER I

What do we mean by differentiation?

If we look back to the early beginnings of formal education – the single room schoolhouse where pupils of all ages and abilities were taught together – differentiation has always been part of educational practice. Perhaps not using sophisticated modern-day pedagogy, specific terminology or indeed the complex psychology of learning, but simply as an often implicit part of teaching that has evolved with the education system. So what is differentiation? To be blunt, there is no one definition of differentiation. However, all current definitions are underpinned by considering learners as individuals and learning as a personalised process. The Training and Development Agency for Schools described differentiation quite succinctly as 'the process by which differences between learners are accommodated so that all students in a group have the best possible chance of learning'. This applies to all classes whether mixed ability or set. It applies to all learners, from those with specific educational needs to the gifted learner. It drives our personalisation of learning to ensure that all pupils make progress and achieve.

The three key aspects of differentiation are based on: readiness to learn (what pupils have already learnt and what are they ready to learn), learning needs (how pupils best learn) and interests (what inspires pupils to learn). This typically entails modifications to our practice and how we develop our lessons to accommodate what can be great variation in and between these parameters. Essentially, if we do not have a strong awareness of an individual pupil's learning context then it is difficult to differentiate. As professionals we will need to address:

- how we design a lesson to maximise pupil progress (process);
- any specific educational needs;
- whether we have any learning support in the classroom;
- the resources that we use (products);
- the content of the lesson;
- the assessment practices used (how we will use prior and on-going assessment data to inform differentiation);
- how we group pupils;
- the learning environment.

There are different ways in which we differentiate in the classroom: by task, by outcome, by resource, by pace, by grouping, by role, by support, by questioning and by assessment. Of course these can and frequently are used in combination and alongside other techniques.

Differentiation by task

Differentiation by task is where we give pupils different tasks (but the same type of activity) to complete according to their ability. For example, this may be three separate worksheets that target low-, middle- and high-attaining pupils (commonly seen in classrooms). All may encompass the same overarching learning outcome but this will be achieved at different depths (perhaps associated with success criteria). There are two key factors when differentiating by task: how you design the task to ensure that all pupils make progress towards learning outcomes, and how pupils are assigned to a given task. Both of these factors are discussed in detail in Chapter 4. It is important to note here that this type of activity is not simply for mixed-ability classes – it is equally valuable in a 'set' environment. Differentiation by task can be used in combination with other differentiation strategies to support learning; what is important is how tasks are tailored to ensure that we do not apply a glass ceiling to learning and limit progress by assigning pupils to a given 'level'.

Some say that differentiation by task is where all pupils are given a single worksheet on which questions get progressively harder. I argue that this is poor practice and that if you use a single worksheet you must use it wisely (this is discussed in detail in Chapter 4). Remember that two pupils of equal ability may work at a different pace; this would mean that the pupil who works more quickly through a worksheet would complete it first – or have the opportunity to work through the more challenging questions – and the pupil who is not as quick would not reach these questions. This limits their progress. They are no less able; they simply work at a slower pace. When teachers use a single worksheet in this way they often assign different paths to different pupils. Consider, however, the typical worksheet. Most have the applied questions at the end. We can differentiate by having different levels of applied question and different routes through the worksheet but often there is limited space and so producing different worksheets is best to ensure that all pupils experience the appropriate mix of questions.

Differentiation by resource

Differentiation by resource is where we give different pupils, or groups of pupils, different resources in order for them to work towards the same learning outcome. This may result in a classroom where some pupils are designing a poster, some producing a newspaper report, some a radio report, some a PowerPoint presentation (and often different work stations are used). The purpose is to allow pupils to use the medium that best allows them to access learning and that best supports progress in learning.

Often when teachers differentiate by resource they accommodate different learning styles. It is important, however, that pupils are exposed to a range of learning resources and not pigeon-holed into one particular style – this can have the opposite effect and ultimately impact on and limit development.

Differentiation by grouping

Differentiation by grouping, and of course combinations thereof, has different aspects. One of the very first questions asked by teachers when we refer to grouping is 'but how do we group?' The concern is typically related to an observed lesson (where the teacher is eager to 'get it right' – sceptical I know!). There is no *correct* answer. Just like everything we do as teachers, what you have to do is think about grouping in the context of the activity and how grouping will best support all pupils to achieve the learning goals. Sometimes it is appropriate for us to group pupils of similar ability and sometimes it is appropriate for us to group pupils of mixed ability. When we group pupils of similar ability most see this as an opportunity for learners to work together at their 'level' and teachers are often comfortable with this concept. When we group by mixed ability some teachers get concerned that the more able pupils are 'held back'. The opposite, however, is true. In such contexts the benefit for more able pupils is that they have to explain – they *teach* others. There is great learning power in this (we discuss this in detail in Chapter 4). In reality, the question we must ask ourselves is the purpose of the grouping – why group in the first place and how does grouping impact on learning? This will help to clarify why we are grouping and how it will maximise progress. Other opportunities for grouping can be based around different learning styles or combined with different resources and these may of course be mixed- or similar-ability groupings. Some pupils may benefit more from an activity (which focuses on the same learning outcome) if they are using new technologies, others if they are using text, others if they are designing a poster and so on, or it may be the specific role that they take within the group (scribe, narrator, chairperson, etc.) that provides the benefit. Grouping pupils in this way allows them to best access learning. There is therefore much more to think about than simply assigning pupils to a group.

Differentiation by pace

Differentiation by pace is exactly as the name suggests. It is effectively the speed with which pupils work through an activity and then progress to the next. Some think that the more able progress quickly through activities (they grasp complex activities at a faster pace). However, in more creative subjects the more able often use time to think more deeply or explore in more depth (they therefore work more slowly, producing work that is of greater length, detail and complexity). Pace can be used to benefit all pupils and, as discussed in Chapter 2, some pupils can follow a single learning cycle and others may follow two or more parallel learning cycles. This allows differentiation by pace to support learning.

Differentiation by outcome

This is where all pupils are given exactly the same task or activity and the same resources. Differentiation is by the differing end points that pupils achieve. In my opinion this is not the best form of differentiation because it is what we are trying to 'get away from' in the classroom (it is exactly what those teachers who do not plan for differentiation in learning do – they give every pupil the same work to complete). It is, however, effective if pupils are conducting an investigation, rich task, research project or an open task, and it is often effective in this context when used in combination with other types of differentiation. The key message is to be cautious if you use differentiation by outcome and ensure that you are indeed differentiating, and that you are using this form of differentiation in the most appropriate context.

Differentiation by support

This is something that teachers do naturally. They target support where it is needed and they interact with pupils to ensure that all pupils are confident in achieving the learning outcomes. It is important, however, that we address the type of support that we offer. This might be differentiation by scaffolding (discussed in Chapters 3, 4 and 5) – where we structure a question to encourage thinking or to construct knowledge – or it may be through the dialogue that we have with pupils (differentiation by dialogue). It is with this dialogue that we need to ensure that we are not 'giving pupils the answer' but that the way in which we interact with pupils encourages them to think independently. As part of this dialogue we might use questioning to develop thinking (typically in this context developing from lower-order to higher-order questions). With the more-able pupils we can further challenge and extend thinking and with the less able use subtle prompts that guide learning (without giving them too much information) – ensuring that our input supports all pupils in making progress. The language we use plays an essential part in differentiating by dialogue in that the vocabulary and complexity of the language we use will vary dependent upon the pupil. A less-able pupil may require a more detailed explanation using simple language when compared with a more-able pupil who is able to engage in more sophisticated discussion. However we interact with pupils, it is absolutely essential that we do so to encourage metacognition.

Working with teaching assistants

Other sources of support in the classroom include learning support assistants or teaching assistants. It is important that if we have teaching assistants in our classroom that we actively engage with them prior to the lesson (during the lesson is far too late and their role will then have limited and less impact). Teaching assistants are professionals but they cannot operate blindly to support pupils in our classroom. We need to ensure that they are aware of how you wish pupils to develop their learning and that they are confident with the topic and resources to be used. Unless we interact with those who support learning in our classrooms we run the risk of them offering too much support too soon and therefore limiting independent development.

Differentiation by questioning

Questioning is discussed in Chapter 7, where we focus on using Bloom's Taxonomy to develop learning – promoting thinking through questioning. Bloom's Taxonomy classifies questions according to their level of cognitive demand (from lower order to higher order). The type of questions we ask and the context in which we ask them is extremely important. Higher-order questions develop deeper learning yet research suggests that we do not ask enough higher-order questions in the classroom. Indeed, when we do, we aim them at the more-able pupils. This limits the progress of the less able – if they are only ever asked lower-order questions then they are not encouraged to extend their thinking beyond lower-order processing. We must therefore carefully design questions that challenge all learners and encourage deeper thinking. Other factors contribute to effective classroom questioning (discussed in Chapter 7) such as, wait time (process and response), how we select pupils to answer and how we develop questioning across the classroom; it is not simply about the type of question that we ask.

Differentiation and OFSTED

It would be remiss not to mention the OFSTED criteria relating to differentiation. While not specifically referred to as 'differentiation', there is reference in the outstanding criteria for ensuring that learning needs are met to ensure progress. Indeed the OFSTED criteria (OFSTED 2014a) states that:

Inspectors must consider whether:

- teaching engages and includes all pupils with work that is challenging enough and that meets the pupils' needs as identified by teachers
- teachers monitor pupils' responses in lessons and adapt their approach accordingly; also, whether they monitor pupils' progress over time and use the information well to adapt their planning
- teachers routinely give the necessary attention to the most able and the disadvantaged, as they do to low-attaining pupils or those who struggle at school
- teachers set homework in line with the school's policy and that challenges all pupils, especially the most able
- assessment is frequent and accurate and is used to set challenging work that builds on prior knowledge, understanding and skills

To achieve an outstanding (1) judgement:

- All teachers have consistently high expectations of all pupils. They plan and teach lessons that enable pupils to learn. As a result, almost all pupils currently on roll in the school, including disabled pupils, those who have special educational needs, disadvantaged pupils and the most able, are making sustained progress that leads to outstanding achievement exceptionally well across the curriculum.

These extracts all point to differentiation in the classroom being essential if we are to create outstanding learning.

High expectations

Expectation is an extremely important part of differentiation; we need to have high expectations of all pupils and challenge each individual to ensure they make optimum progress. Where differentiation won't work to best effect is when we categorise pupils according to a predetermined ability and this is one of the concerns when teachers differentiate by using data ineffectively – essentially they categorise pupils according to prior data or target grades and then label them as low-, middle- or high-attaining (which tends to stick). In pre-assigning pupils to a specific classification (effectively pre-planning learning) we potentially apply a glass ceiling to some pupils. Those pupils to whom we assign to the 'low' category have lower expectations of themselves and even given choice they will select the 'low' ability option (perhaps the easy option) because this has been conditioned. We need to prevent this labelling of pupils (discussed in Chapter 6). It is important that we use assessment for learning during the lesson to inform next steps. For example, while a pupil may, in general, be middle-attaining they might excel in one particular area and yet require further support in another. Using formative assessment during learning is essential to ensure that we use differentiation in the most effective way to develop, challenge and extend learning. We discuss the close relationship between differentiation and assessment for learning in Chapter 6.

Summary

Differentiation is not an isolated practice. Some channels of differentiation are carefully planned – particularly when planning activities. Others occur simply as a consequence of the direction learning takes during the lesson (which can't necessarily be pre-planned such as, for example, differentiation through bounce-back questioning or support). However we choose to differentiate learning in the lesson, we need to ensure that the method we use will benefit learning and enhance the learning experience for all pupils. Explicit differentiation is not always necessary – what is more important is that you think carefully about how an activity will allow pupils to make progress. Investing in teacher training is key to improving teaching and learning. Without high quality training teachers will struggle to interpret the many policies that are imposed on them. Differentiation is no exception. Teachers need training on how to differentiate learning and how to combine this with the other pedagogical strategies they use in the classroom to create an outstanding learning environment.

In this book we take the lesson structure and focus on how to differentiate activities at various stages of learning. The important point is that there is no one-size-fits-all approach. The very purpose of differentiation is personalisation and this cannot be downplayed. How you differentiate will depend wholly on your audience. Taking three different worksheets one teacher has designed for their class will not necessarily automatically work for your class. Sharing resources is important (there is little point in reinventing the wheel), but more important is tailoring them to the individuals in your classroom. It is also important to remember that not everything works first time. Sometimes things that we think will go really well simply don't. The message is not to give up – keep trying until you find what works for you and the pupils in your classroom. One outstanding teacher can teach very differently from another. There is no single model that we must all follow – the key is that all pupils make progress and this is where differentiation is essential.

Sequencing and planning for learning

The order and organisation of learning activities affects the way information is processed and retained. It isn't simply about progressing from a simple to a complex activity but about the prerequisite skills and cognitive processes involved. To allow all pupils to achieve the learning outcomes, different approaches to learning are needed and we need to be flexible in how we develop our lessons. This is why differentiation needs to be an implicit part of our planning. When we use the word 'plan' it doesn't mean we write a rigid tick list of activities that we expect pupils to complete if they are to achieve the learning outcomes (a task-driven, outcome-oriented approach). We need to be flexible – when we plan for learning we need to consider the different branches that learning may take and we should always be aware of any potential pitfalls and misconceptions that may develop – thinking about how we may support pupils in overcoming any hurdles. An essential part of this process is how we develop thinking and support cognitive development.

I make reference to different phases in the lesson (the start, main body and plenary) and indeed dedicate specific chapters to each (Chapters 3, 4 and 5 respectively). However, I do not advocate a rigid or explicit three-part lesson structure. I use these terms because many teachers can relate to them and are able to then translate the concepts we discuss to their daily practice. It is important to remember that however you structure learning, the lesson should flow and each activity should build in some way on the previous supporting progressive development. We do not explicitly segment our lesson (completing a starter activity, main activity and plenary as independent sections) – we develop activities that connect and progress learning. While it is true that some activities lend themselves best to the start of the lesson or to the main body of the lesson, where we approach learning in a different way, it is how we sequence learning and the emphasis we place on different parts of the learning cycle that is most important.

Sequenced learning cycles underpin a lesson that develops progress in learning. Each phase of the lesson consists of one or more learning cycles and each section of the cycle can be of varying length. In some lessons, for example, the more able may develop learning through a single learning cycle (with greater focus on concept development) and those who require more support may develop their learning through two or more sequenced learning cycles, which allow them to make progress towards the same learning outcomes over a parallel period. It is important to note at this stage, when planning for differentiation, that we do not create an unmanageable classroom with so many different pathways or potential learning options that we lose the potential benefit of a differentiated learning environment. When you plan for learning keep in mind the overarching learning outcome and the success criteria. Plan the lesson initially around this – with activities in mind. Once you have decided on a particular activity that will best achieve the learning purpose then you can think about how you may choose to differentiate that activity to ensure that all pupils benefit from the experience. It might be that some pupils follow one or more learning cycles or that some pupils use different resources or work in a group. Remember that this is not for the whole lesson and that there will be times that it might be inappropriate to differentiate. Differentiation supports learning and should be used to enhance pupil progress but, at the same time, we need to think sensibly about differentiation in our classrooms and how we manage learning to ensure the best possible outcomes for all pupils – this is a fine balance.

The activities we use are an essential part of the differentiation process. Do they suit the learning needs of our pupils? Can all pupils access the activity? Do we need to tailor the activity to different learners to ensure they can make progress? How is the activity assessed? Does assessment inform next steps? Does assessment inform different learning pathways? These simple questions need to become second nature when planning a lesson. If you aren't addressing these types of question, then most likely you are planning for teaching. In other words you are planning the activities that you will teach (the focus is on you) and you are thinking about how you will impose this knowledge *on* pupils (information or content delivery) rather than focusing on developing pupils' learning and, consequently, their independent thinking skills. Planning for learning is very different to planning for teaching. When we plan for learning we immediately think about our audience. We shift the focus from us to the pupils in our classroom – how they are going to access and develop a particular topic – we focus on them and on how we can support them in making progress. A simple tip is to focus on what you want pupils to achieve (the learning outcomes) and think back to pupils' starting points. Then think carefully about how you are going to sequence activities to support pupils in getting from their starting point to the desired outcome (these end points may be different for different individuals). Are there any hurdles to overcome? Are there any potential misconceptions? Which activities best develop learning? If we start at the beginning and plan openly we can branch in too many directions so, to remain focused, concentrate on the outcomes and then effectively work backwards.

The learning cycle

You will, no doubt, have been introduced to learning cycles at some point during your teaching career. There are many different learning cycles – the commonality is that they are all based on the psychology of learning. Our job is to translate theory into practice. It is therefore important to make any theory relevant to you and the learners in your classroom. I always keep in mind the learning cycle illustrated in Figure 2.1, which consists of four sections: developing the concept, activating learning, embedding learning and reflection. This is how I structure learning in my classroom and the learning cycle that I feel is most appropriate to secure progress. It is important to remember that effective learning only occurs when a learner is able to execute all four stages of the model (irrespective of the model that you use or the number of stages it has). No one stage of the cycle is effective as a learning procedure on its own and, while you may start at any point in the cycle, learners must progress through each stage.

The amount of time you dedicate to each specific stage of the model will depend upon many different factors: learning style, attitudes to learning, cognitive ability, learner preference, learner choice, learner's interests, the specific activity, and so on. A cycle may be over a series of lessons, a single lesson or many sequential cycles may occur in one lesson and indeed cycles within cycles. It is a complicated process and the aim here is not to delve into the psychology of learning or how the brain processes information but to think about how you can use the learning cycle to ensure all learners develop. Figure 2.2 and Figure 2.3 are examples of how learning cycles may operate in a given lesson (often individual learning cycles secure one or more success criteria) – there may be one learning cycle in the main or several learning cycles or one cycle encompassing several mini-cycles. Different pupils may follow different pathways.

It is also important to keep in mind the amount of information we are asking pupils to process at any one time. Research suggests that our brains can only handle between five and nine (inclusive) discrete pieces of information at once (Miller, 1968). This magical number (seven plus or minus two) is often interpreted as the number of objects we can hold in our working memory. Some information though

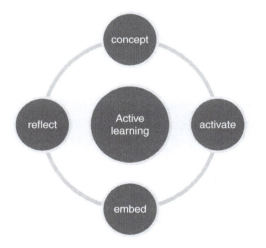

Figure 2.1 The learning cycle.

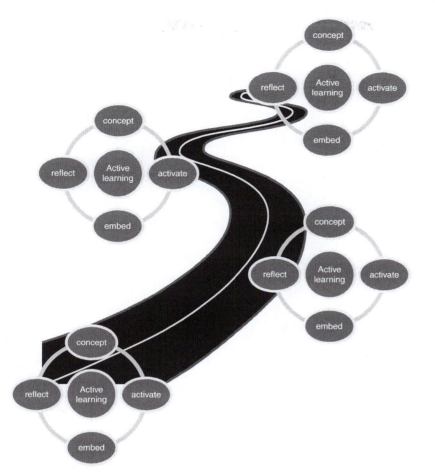

Figure 2.2 The learning journey.

is easier to retain than others – because of prior knowledge or previous association. If we ask a non-chemist to remember the following chemical formulae, NaClO, $(NH_4)_2SO_4$ and $CuSO_4$, they would most likely be unable to recall it correctly (to them it is simply a sequence of letters and numbers and has no meaning). However, a chemist would be able to recall the formulae with ease – by drawing on prior knowl-edge or word association such as, for example, sodium hypochlorite, ammonium sulphate and copper sulphate – processing the information as though it were com-prised of fewer units. Simply recalling the six words they can translate these back to chemical symbols when asked. We would be expecting a non-chemist to remember 19 items (words, numbers and symbols) that appear to be random to their brain (no connections or associations can be made) in the correct order. Therefore, the same information could 'overload' one individual but not another. This is why we must chunk learning and structure learning to consider how much we are expecting pupils

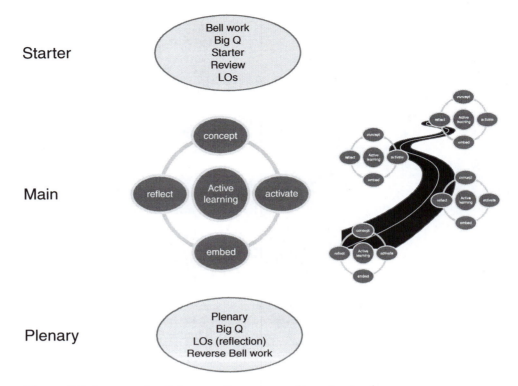

Figure 2.3 An example of the overall sequence of learning in a lesson.

to process and the basis for this learning. Knowledge of the individual pupil and their learning background can ensure that we differentiate to support progress.

As a consequence of the fact that we have 30 individuals with different experiences in our classrooms at any one time, we have to be prepared to detour at any point; even the best-planned lessons will not necessarily go to plan. This may mean that you interject and guide learning in a specific phase to support pupils in the process (differentiation through support – something that often cannot be planned). If this is the case it is still important to ensure that all stages of the cycle are completed. Remember that learning is not a smooth journey and there are many ups and downs. Those ups and downs inform our next steps. What is important is that pupils make progress and, of course, this will be at different rates (pace is a key part of differentiation in learning and we must ensure that it does not impede the progress of a more-able pupil who may work at a slower rate to an equivalent peer). Our job is to ensure that activities are accessible for all (without doing this learning will simply not happen or, worse still, will negate any previous progress) and this is why differentiation is so important. In the remainder of this chapter we consider the different stages of the learning cycle and what these mean in the context of the classroom.

Stages of the learning cycle

Cognitive engagement occurs in the 'active' and 'concept' stages of the cycle. It is where pupils think about thinking. They develop their own learning through cleverly sequenced activities that allow them to investigate and to explore different ideas, challenging their own learning and the learning of others, developing their questioning and encouraging higher order thinking skills. This is in contrast to compliance tasks where pupils might be engaged with a task, but not necessarily learning. Think carefully about the difference between the two. A pupil can be engaged with a task (i.e. completing it and this 'doing' can be mistaken for engagement) but not be learning – they could simply be applying a method that they have been 'taught' rather than understanding the method that they are using. These types of activities used in isolation generally access only lower-order thinking skills and are often used in lessons that follow the 'I do, you do, we do' style where the teacher demonstrates a method and then pupils effectively recall and use this recipe to complete a series of questions (so thinking can be easily overlooked). Think about baking a cake. If I give you a recipe and you follow it to the letter you will no doubt produce beautiful cakes. If, however, I begin to challenge your thinking and ask you why, for example, we use particular ingredients or why we do things in a certain way, or I ask you to apply the recipe or adapt it to a different context, you may not be able to answer or do so. This does not impede your ability to produce the cakes but it does demonstrate that you can make the cakes (complete the activity) without any real understanding of the process (i.e. you are using lower-order skills). We must therefore be conscious of this in our teaching. This is not to say that compliance activities have no place in the classroom. Combined with the active and concept phases of the cycle compliance activities serve to embed the concepts that pupils have developed, allowing pupils to apply their learning. It is this application of learning that moves to higher-order thinking skills. Pupils have the opportunity to embed the concepts that they have developed and it is this, combined with the other stages of the learning cycle, that means compliance tasks can support learning. In isolation as an activity they serve little purpose in enhancing learning and this is why I emphasise again that no one phase of the learning cycle is effective on its own.

In the reflective phase of the cycle pupils reflect on their learning. They process their thoughts and consolidate, which allows them to inform their next steps and to make choices. We learn not only from our experiences but also from our mistakes, and we deepen learning by reflecting on these. Without the process of actively thinking about those experiences, and questioning ourselves about what they mean, learning doesn't really happen. Therefore, in reflecting on learning at key points in the lesson we allow pupils to synthesise. Pupils need to think about what they have been doing, how and why. It is an opportunity for them to challenge themselves further, identify what they did well, key areas for development and to formulate any questions they may need to ask of themselves, their peers or teaching staff. Reflection is an important part of the learning cycle and at different phases of the lesson it may have different durations (for example, in the plenary more time is usually dedicated to activities of this type). It is where assessment for learning supports development. Reflection is so often either rushed or not completed at all (because time runs out) and yet it is crucial to learning, so be conscious that reflection forms a key part of learning in your classroom and ensure that it is of high quality. It is not simply a case of 'what have I learnt today' and this is discussed in detail in Chapter 5.

'We do not learn from experience...we learn from reflecting on experience' (John Dewey). I want to take a moment to think a little about how we introduce concepts (we address this fully in Chapter 4). Pupils need to think independently (albeit with our guidance) and one of the things teachers often revert back to in classrooms is 'teacher talk'. They talk at pupils far too much. The key word here being 'at'. I use the example of my journey to work (Bartlett, 2014). If I talk at you and tell you about my journey to work then, after a few minutes, you would most likely switch off and when I question you about my journey to work you would be unlikely to answer the questions.

> Today I drove to work. I took road X because road Y was closed due to a burst water pipe. This meant I was taking the longer route. As I drove down road Y I considered my next move. I wanted to take the shortest route so I took road B and then took the first right down road C. This meant I ended up on road M....

Pretty boring! Now consider if I give you a map. I then give you a few statements such as, 'road Y is closed due to a burst water pipe', and so on. I also provide you with information on the length of each road and drop in some statements like 'I want to take the shortest route where possible'. If I then ask you to piece together all of the information and draw my route on the map (in this case there is only one possible outcome), and then ask you about my journey, you would be far more likely to be able to recount the route and to explain why I drove this route. Why? Simply because you were involved in the process. Involving pupils in learning is one of the fundamental purposes of the learning cycle. When we involve pupils in their own learning we are much more likely to develop higher-order thinkers, pupils who are able to apply learning to different contexts and who can justify and explain their thoughts (reasoned argument).

Taking this one step further, now reflect on your own practice. It is important to think very carefully about where you would place yourself on the line shown in Figure 2.4. At the same time answer the following questions:

* Is this the same every lesson?
* Is it the same for each class or does it depend on 'what you are doing'?
* Does it vary within a class when you work with different groups of pupils?
* Does it depend on 'when' you are teaching the group (compare first thing Monday morning to the last period on a Friday afternoon)?

There is a fine balance to be achieved between the two. Often teachers will differentiate by giving more-able pupils the more active (right-hand extreme) activities

Where are you on the active learning spectrum?

| Quiet, compliant tasks (lots of worksheet-style/individual driven activities) | Active and engaging learning environment (collaborative learning opportunities) |

Figure 2.4 The learning line.

and the less able the more compliant tasks. When they do this they tend to instruct the less able – show them how to do something and then expect them to complete a worksheet for example. This is of course not good practice in differentiation. In fact it limits progress (this is the 'I do, you do, we do' style of teaching – think back to the baking example discussed earlier in this chapter) and limits the thinking that pupils do. All pupils need to be exposed to a mixture of the two activities and, for your 'normal' daily practice, aim to be somewhere in the middle of the spectrum – using a variety of different activities to support learning. Where differentiation comes into play is not necessarily in the type of activity but how we structure that activity (like, for example, using scaffolding) and this is discussed in detail in Chapters 3, 4 and 5.

A further example of poor practice is when teachers differentiate by behaviour and give pupils who are potentially more challenging (in terms of behaviour) the compliant tasks. They force the worksheet-type activity on them in an attempt to prevent interaction between pupils and limit behavioural problems. This can, of course, have the opposite effect. Those pupils who exhibit low-level disruptive behaviour often do so because they are 'bored'. They need to be more actively involved in their learning and, yes, that means making noise (and there is nothing wrong with this as long as the noise is learning noise). Teachers worry about a lack of control when they move towards the right of the spectrum but, if you carefully manage your classroom and have clear expectations for behaviour and rules for regaining attention (for example, 'one, two, three, eyes on me'), then implementing these types of activity should engage learners and ensure they make progress (they might even enjoy learning!) – reducing low level disruptive behaviour. This doesn't happen overnight and it needs careful development. You can't have every activity at the extreme. So, to begin with, plan a short-burst activity and then see how it goes. You have to be prepared for failure and to persevere – it is how you reflect on your own practice and how you then evaluate and act upon this that develops you as a practitioner. Best practice does not happen overnight. Outstanding teachers are not born outstanding – they carefully craft and adapt their practice.

The reason we differentiate is to make learning accessible to all. Indeed accessibility is a factor in disengagement and this is the case across all ability levels. Remember that all pupils are individuals – they think differently, have different life experiences and their brain processes things in a way unique to them (they are not simply data on a school management system and no one individual is the same). How we perceive things can alter our conscious ability to embrace new learning. As teachers we need to open different doors – inspiring pupils and creating a state of curiosity in learning. I often use the illustrations shown in Figures 2.5, 2.6 and 2.7 when working with teachers to demonstrate that:

*   how we 'see' the same thing can be very different;
*   our fundamental processing skills are at different rates.

Figure 2.5 A famous perceptual illusion in which the brain switches between seeing an old lady or a young woman.
Note: This image is believed to have been adapted by W. E. Hill and published in *Puck* magazine in 1915 (Hill, 1915) although the image is believed to have originated from an anonymous German postcard in 1888.

Figure 2.6 A perceptual illusion showing two faces from one perspective or a vase from another (www.shutterstock.com).

Figure 2.7 A perceptual illusion showing columns from one perspective or two women talking from another (www.shutterstock.com).

In each of these optical illusions the picture is, of course, the same but how your brain processes the image changes how you 'see' it and, consequently, your immediate reaction to it and, indeed, this is much the same as learning. How we perceive something can change how we react to it. If pupils think something is too hard or 'beyond them' then they will disengage but if we make that learning accessible by providing them with a different 'view' then we can change their attitude to learning. It's all about making learning accessible and this is where differentiation and assessment are crucial – the two go hand in hand. Frustration arises when we can't do something or when we can't understand the 'why'.

The rate at which we change our perception and are able to 'see' the alternative also impacts on learning. This differs greatly – some people 'just can't see it' and others gradually see the alternative at a different pace (for example, interchanging between the old lady and the young lady in Figure 2.5). This is similar to how pupils are able to embrace new concepts and ideas or to take a different viewpoint. We must be very aware that pupils process things at different rates but the rate of process does not make someone any less able. It is important to be conscious of how we are guiding pupils to the changing view. In many cases telling them 'it is there' (as with the image) doesn't mean they will 'see' it – this goes back to how we engage learners with developing new concepts; their active involvement in learning. If you immediately *see* the young woman in Figure 2.5, just because I *tell* you that it is also an image of an old woman doesn't mean you will *see* it. Be conscious of this when planning for learning and when interacting with pupils.

To conclude I want to make reference to a famous quote in *Winnie-the-Pooh* (Milne, 1926) (the accompanying illustration is wonderful) – the one where Edward Bear is being bumped down the stairs behind Christopher Robin. Edward Bear thinks this is the only way, as far as he knows, of coming down the stairs but, for a split second, he considers the possibility that there *might* be another way - if he was just given the opportunity to stop and think for a moment. But Christopher Robin continues to bump Edward Bear down the stairs in the same way – leaving no time for thinking. This continued and repeated action leads Edward Bear to conclude that being bumped down the stairs behind Christopher Robin must of course be the only way. If Christopher is doing it that way then it must be right, so he stops thinking. He gives up and accepts it – as if he shouldn't have been (or was silly to be) thinking in the first place. The reason I make reference to this extract is because it is how many pupils feel about learning. They accept that 'this is the way to do something' irrespective of whether they understand it. Why? Because the teacher has told them this is 'how we do it' and, since the teacher is seen to be the expert, then this must be the only way. They stop questioning – analogous to Edward Bear being bumped down the stairs. The result is that learning is compliant and functional. We often see the asking of 'why' diminished as a pupil progresses through our education system. Look to a primary classroom or pupils of a young age outside of the classroom – you will hear them asking 'why'. They are curious and they don't just accept what we tell them (we often hear 'yes, but why?'). As pupils get older (think about the senior school classroom) we hear pupils asking 'why' far less often – they become conditioned to being 'told' and to following instructions (they implicitly believe what we tell them). The state of curiosity (sadly) is far less. To engage learners and to make learning accessible so that all pupils can make progress we must embrace the learning cycle and use each stage to develop and secure learning. Differentiation supports progress and we need to encourage pupils to think of different possibilities, to take different routes, to ask 'why' and to challenge and explore learning.

Summary

No one person learns in the same way as another. There are similarities but pupils are individuals; internal and external factors shape their learning profiles. We are typically faced with 30 different pupils in a class and when we teach five classes a day that is potentially 150 individuals through our door. It would be impossible to expect us to plan 150 personalised learning pathways but what we can do is to use the learning cycle to allow pupils to explore learning and to shape their own journey (involving them in learning). We are there to support that process and to act as guides at each stage. The key factor is to ensure that all stages of the learning cycle are completed – they do not operate in isolation and that learning is accessible for all. 'The whole is greater than the sum of its parts' (Aristotle).

When you plan an activity use the following as a guide:

- What is the overarching learning outcome?
- What are the success criteria at key learning points?
- Are pupils aware of the learning outcome and success criteria and do they understand them?
- What are pupils' individual starting points?
- Where are we starting on the learning cycle?
- How will each stage of the learning cycle inform the next?
- Have I planned to ensure that all stages are completed?
- Can all pupils access the activity?
- What supporting mechanisms are in place?
- Have I allowed sufficient time for reflection and made this part of the learning process?
- Are pupils aware of the next steps in their learning journey?

CHAPTER 3

Differentiation for learning: the start of the lesson

The starter activity is recognised as having a significant impact on the quality of learning, not only at the beginning of the lesson but during the lesson as a whole. It is our opportunity to 'hook' learners and actively engage them in learning from the moment they enter the classroom. Whether you differentiate a starter activity or not and how you may or may not do this very much depends on where you are in the learning process. Indeed, before you think about differentiating it is important to focus on the purpose of the starter activity. Be very clear about pupils' learning and about the information it provides, both to you as a leader of learning and to pupils as owners of their own learning. If, for example, a starter activity is used to benchmark learning then it is advisable for all pupils to do the same activity and to use the results of this activity to differentiate learning as the lesson progresses (informing the next steps). On the other hand, if the lesson sits in a series of lessons where learning builds on recent prior knowledge, which will potentially have developed at different depths, and we wish to make connections in learning, then it is sensible to use your assessment of prior learning to differentiate the starter activity and match the activity to the needs of the learners (this does not imply solely differentiation by ability). The essence being that what is most important is to think very carefully about the learning purpose of each activity and, while there may be differing opinions on this, I believe (given the reality of learning in the classroom and the busy day-to-day of teachers) we must remember that it is not always necessary nor indeed appropriate to differentiate each and every activity.

Differentiation is used to support learning and should be a platform for maximising pupil progress. It is not an isolated practice. Indeed assessment for learning and differentiation for learning work in tandem. High-quality assessment informs differentiation and high-quality differentiation improves assessment outcomes. Of course alongside this is behaviour management. Teachers are often concerned about behaviour when there are different groups of pupils simultaneously doing different activities because there is a perceived lack of control and a concern that having concurrent activities can potentially descend into chaos. It is true that this requires careful management and planning but it is worth addressing at this point that low-level disruption in classrooms is often through pupils not being engaged in learning or where they cannot access learning. Best practice in differentiation, supported by high-quality assessment for learning, should minimise this. In this chapter we look at differentiation for learning in the context of the starter activity, discussing the importance of assessment and of linking all aspects of the learning cycle. We must always be conscious that when we differentiate we do not simply do so by ability grouping as this can limit the progress of learners. Differentiation is far more than this and an awareness of different types of differentiation is important to enhance learning and to ensure we do not pigeonhole pupils and apply a glass ceiling to progress.

Bell work

Bell work is a short activity that bridges the gap between pupils arriving to your lesson and the lesson formally beginning. We know from experience that pupils' arrival at lessons can be staggered (often three minutes or more) and bell work prevents this valuable learning time being wasted. The activity itself occupies pupils during this short period and emphasises the importance of the classroom being a place of learning. It also gives you the opportunity to set up your lesson, which is particularly useful if you move from classroom to classroom or if you teach lesson after lesson and as one class is leaving another arrives – you can then start the first learning activity (the starter) when you are ready.

Bell work itself is not a starter activity and so it is important to pitch the activity at an appropriate level that engages pupils and allows all pupils to access the activity independently. The key word is 'independently'. Often teachers make this activity the same for all pupils (and there is nothing wrong with this). However, it provides an ideal opportunity to differentiate and to target learning. For example, if your previous assessment data shows that pupil X needs further practice on fractions and pupil Y needs further practice on solving equations then you may write two simple questions on a post-it for each pupil to return to you at the end of the lesson. Whether you differentiate in this way or not remember that bell work is brief and is not a starter activity so, ideally, it should last no longer than a couple of minutes. What you do not want to do is create a situation where bell work leads to an in-depth discussion and, before you know it, you are 20 minutes into the lesson. Also remember that bell work does not have to link to learning in the lesson so it really is an ideal opportunity to check-in with pupils on their progress with other areas that they may need reminding of and it gives you evidence of their progress in learning. Some pupils need short regular practice on specific topics and bell work is an opportunity for this. A lot of mathematics teachers say that pupils 'don't like' fractions (and indeed if you ask many adults the topic they least enjoyed in mathematics when they were at school it will no doubt be fractions) and if it is left as an isolated topic 'taught a few months ago' it becomes remote from their learning pattern and a distant memory. When I use bell work to support practice with fractions on a regular basis pupils are much more confident in approaching what is often an unpopular topic and they are much more able to transfer and apply their skills to other areas of mathematics. This is worth keeping in mind when you plan bell work activities and it really is an ideal opportunity to personalise learning – if we are honest how long does it really take to jot a quick question on a post-it for each pupil? Remember this does not have to be done every lesson – for some lessons you might use a generic bell-work question – but it is important to mix it up and occasional use of personalised problems really does create a personalised learning experience and pupils know that you are focusing on their individual development.

I always emphasise that if behaviour management is a concern then it is best to use a settling activity, with more active bell work used as pupils become more confident or you are comfortable with the environment that it creates. A few simple questions on the board (electronic or otherwise) as pupils arrive works really well and helps to reinforce subject matter (and, as stated above, we know that increasing exposure to topics on a regular basis helps to embed learning), and the post-it note or individual piece of paper works well to personalise learning. My advice is not to assess the bell work activity at the start of the lesson (as this can ultimately increase the amount of time dedicated to this simple activity) but to leave assessment until the final minute or so of the lesson and assess the activity through reverse bell work. By ensuring that you always review the bell work at the end of the lesson you add value to the activity and pupils soon become aware that they can't simply avoid the bell work activity (by arriving a few minutes late for example) but need to be involved as soon as they enter the classroom. Even those arriving late are involved in the reverse bell work review (give those who may not have had chance to complete their task a minute to do so at the end of the lesson or add it to the homework) so there is no opportunity for avoidance.

Listed below are some short examples of different types of bell work across a variety of subjects. The examples used are designed to demonstrate the ease with which bell work activities can be generated, ensuring that incorporating them into a lesson is not an onerous task. For each activity I will discuss opportunities for differentiation.

Recall of fact

Recall activities use lower-order cognitive skills and, as such, are a good basis for bell work. They remind pupils of certain topics, can be used to reinforce different content for individuals (often useful closer to examinations) and rely at this stage on little or no teacher input, making them ideal as independent activities. Regular practise of these sorts of tasks improves recall and basic knowledge skills, strengthening the foundations of learning. Differentiation of recall activities can be done in many different ways. For example, all pupils might be given the same topic but asked different content-based questions or questions at different levels of challenge. There is also the option to personalise this activity further by giving groups or individuals different topics based upon areas for development highlighted in previous assessment activities or, alternatively, presenting the question in different ways (perhaps through diagrams or imagery or other medium). This might not be something that you do every lesson (preparation time can be greater if personalising in this way) but may be something you do following an assessment or closer to an examination.

Examples of differentiating topics are given below:

- Mathematics: if pupils are struggling with solving equations then, depending upon the skills pupils need to develop and the stage they are in their learning, you may ask one pupil to solve equations of the nature $2x + 3 = 11$ and another to solve equations with the unknown on both sides such as $5x - 7 = 12x + 4$. Those pupils who are still struggling with the 'balance' concept may be given a balancing diagram to complete or, alternatively, the more able a question in context. The underlying skill or process used is the same and the reverse bell work would draw out this discussion.
- Modern foreign languages (MFL): in modern foreign language lessons (instructions given in the target language) this may, perhaps, involve activities such as:

  a) Jumbled sentences – pupils place the jumbled words in the correct order to produce a sentence and then translate. This can be differentiated by asking some pupils to write a 'what could come next' statement or simply by giving different groups jumbled sentences at differing degrees of difficulty. Indeed, for some pupils, you may support learning with illustrations providing a visual aid.

  b) Describing an image – if you ask pupils to describe an image then some can be asked to do this with no support and for others you may offer several adjectives and ask pupils to circle which best describes the object or, conversely, give pupils a series of adjectives and ask them which image is being described. An activity such as this also provides natural differentiation in terms of the adjectives that pupils generate (differentiation by outcome).

- History: if we ask pupils to categorise primary and secondary sources then we can differentiate learning by using different items. For the more-able pupils these items may be more challenging and cause them to think a little deeper. The underlying concept or understanding of how we classify a source as primary or secondary (in other words recall of the definition) is being used by all pupils but we differentiate through the level of challenge (differentiation by task) and how pupils apply this knowledge. You may choose to highlight a few items from each activity to assess learning and to demonstrate how we classify sources. The whole-class discussion at the end of the lesson involves all pupils and can highlight key features.

These are a few simple examples but you can begin to see how one topic can be differentiated with little burden on teacher time. The key point is to keep it brief and something that pupils can work on independently.

'Odd one out'

'Odd one out' activities when used as bell work are best kept short and simple. They require greater depth of thought than the basic recall activities and are useful as a discussion tool in which pupils develop the art of debate (particularly where you use items where the odd one out is not obvious). The power in the activity is pupils thinking about the 'why' or the 'why not' and then being able to explain this. Simply circling an 'odd one out' has little impact on learning without the surrounding discussion. Differentiation of this type of activity is typically through the degree of challenge, although you can use images or objects instead of words to support different learning styles. For example, in technology use different types of wood or materials and ask pupils the odd one out or use different images in art. In physics you may have different circuit boards (two that are complete and one that is incomplete where pupils have to determine the odd one out but also think about why it is incomplete and therefore how to make it complete). Realistically, whatever you choose it needs to be kept simple for bell work and reviewed only at the end of the lesson (reverse bell work) – pace is extremely important. This type of activity is discussed in more detail in the section below titled 'Benchmarking learning' as, in extended form, it makes for an excellent starter or indeed activity in the main or plenary. The purpose for bell work is 'short and sweet' – keep this focus or the activity will drift.

'What if' and 'if' statements

'What if' statements allow for natural differentiation and work well as short statements in bell work, but also act as starter activities leading in to a new learning experience or to develop a particular skill. The underlying question may seem to be a 'bit of fun' but the development in thinking skills should not be underestimated. Examples include:

> 'What if we could fly?'
> 'What if we could see through walls?'
> 'What if we were each given £1 million?'
> 'What if the telephone was never invented?'
> 'What if the internet were shut down for a day?'
> 'What if Romeo and Juliet had never met?'
> 'What if penicillin had not been discovered?'
> 'What if all forms of social media were banned?'
> 'What if tomorrow there were no plants?'

The idea is to promote discussion, reasoned and structured argument and communication skills and this can be addressed during reverse bell work. Differentiation here is natural and occurs through pupil outcomes but the debate that ensues is often interesting. If this is a skill that you wish to develop in a lesson or over a period then use this activity as a starter that links in some way to the learning, where new skills acquired during the lesson may contribute to a 'before' and 'after' comparative argument. In other words, pupils can formulate opinions based on 'originally I thought this....' and by the end of the lesson 'my opinion changed because...'. Alternatively, they may be used to connect learning and a question such as 'what if penicillin had not been discovered?' may form bell work for the lesson following one that has focused on medicine through time or, indeed, a science lesson on antibiotics acting as a connector of learning. For some pupils you may expect a free and formulated response with no support and for others you may differentiate by offering three different statements or scenarios from which they have to select their answer and then justify their choice. This essentially differentiates the activity through scaffolding (by support) as we want all pupils to be able to complete this activity in a similarly short period of time (usually two or three minutes maximum).

'If…' statements involve pupils identifying a connection that is then applied to a problem in a similar context. While this type of activity can be used for bell work it is also an activity that can be used at any point in the lesson as a mini-challenge. For example: 'if $ab = 35$, what are the possible values of a and b (a and b are integers)?' Here we are encouraging pupils to think about number (pairs such as 1 and 35, 5 and 7 but also –1 and –35, –5 and –7). It reinforces both multiplication and the relationship between positive and negative numbers. This is a similar exercise to '"24" – how many ways can we make "24" using a set of three given integers (e.g. 2, 3 and 4)?' A further example commonly used in mathematics is: 'if $6 \times 70 = 420$ then calculate:

1) 0.6×70
2) 6×7000
3) 0.6×0.7
4) $420 / 70$
5) -6×-0.7'

Again, in this example pupils are practising a skill (manipulation of number) and, used frequently (perhaps every two weeks), this helps to embed the concept and has a significant impact on learning.

In English, an example relating to word endings is illustrated below (taken from Bartlett, 2015):

If we add a suffix to words ending in *y* we need to first look at the letter in front of the *y*. If it is a vowel we keep the *y* and if it is a consonant the *y* changes to an *i* and if we add –*ing* the *y* always stays. Based only on this statement write the following correctly:

1) I was *enjoing* watching the movie and I didn't hear the telephone.
2) I am *hungryer* than a horse.

To extend this activity you can ask pupils to determine a simple rule: 'If taste → tasting, heat → heating, place → placing, time → timing, meet → meeting. What is the rule?'

A similar activity can be used in MFL with regular verb endings to encourage pupils to recall and apply a rule. This can be extended to a starter activity if you ask pupils to identify the regular verb endings given different examples of verbs in a given tense. Questions that ask pupils whether they agree or disagree with a statement are another example of this type of bell work: 'Oliver says 27 is greater than 7 so 0.27 is greater than 0.7. Do you agree?'

Being provided with information and then applying this to a new problem is a key skill in all subject areas and increasingly popular in terms of assessing and developing pupils' ability to apply their learning rather than simply recalling facts. While it may seem a rather trivial exercise it does promote higher-order thinking skills when we focus on the 'why'. This allows us to assess whether pupils understand the underlying concepts or whether they are simply applying a 'recipe'. In terms of differentiating this type of activity the obvious method is by task – giving different pupils different 'if' statements to consider (some giving pupils more information than others). Alternatively, these statements can be used in such a way as to encourage pupils to write down any questions they asked themselves such as, whether they require more information, if there are any exceptions to the rule, and so on. Bell work used in this way acts as thought provokers – generating questions that can be returned to at any point during the lesson (in this way the bell work obviously links to the learning in the lesson). The questions themselves allow you to assess cognitive ability and direct future learning – pupils generating similar questions might be grouped together and so on. Remember, used as a standalone, bell work activity discussion happens at the end of the lesson and this is where we review any questions. If this becomes a starter activity then discussion follows the activity.

Other types of bell work

Bell work really can be any activity as long as it is short and does not require your input. Remember that the purpose is to occupy pupils from the moment they enter the classroom, during the brief period where you are greeting pupils as they arrive to the lesson. Some teachers prefer an active start to their lesson and they place posters, objects or images around the room and ask pupils to, for example, go and stand by the one that they find most interesting or the person they think is most important in history. Only during reverse bell work is there any discussion surrounding pupil choice. Differentiating this type of activity is obviously limited to the outcome of any such discussion and then through targeted questioning and, while it may seem an abstract activity, it can be used to remind pupils of key facts. For example, you might place different food sources around the classroom and ask pupils which would provide you with the most energy. The focus during the reverse bell work is on the comparison between different foods and food groups and, equally, on pupils' ability to identify different food groups and their properties. Alternatively, you may be studying Macbeth and ask pupils to go and stand by their favourite character. A few minutes before the end of the lesson you can ask pupils to return to their character and, in the small groups that will naturally form, they have to list three key features of the character. What this does is promote thinking skills in a different and perhaps less formal working context (the results of this type of activity are valuable). In this way the bell work activity links to the learning in the lesson (the text of Macbeth) and it may be that you revisit the bell work choice during the lesson and use this as a platform for discussion. What factors influenced their choice? Will their decision stay the same or after further work in the lesson does it now change? This type of activity can also be used as a starter activity in extended form. This may include new character groups, where pupils focus collectively on the characteristics of the person they chose. At key points in the lesson they re-form and decide whether the individual remains their choice and if so why.

Other examples include using a washing line and asking pupils to place items in a specific order. This may be organising events in chronology, ordering decimals, fractions and percentages in order of size, sequencing a chemical reaction or experiment, or placing the process of photosynthesis in order. You may choose to differentiate this activity by having, for example, three washing lines and allocating pupils to a specific area/zone (differentiating by group, which may be mixed ability, or differentiating by similar ability groupings with different levels of challenge) or choose to leave one card blank for pupils to fill in. They then work as a team. This does, however, need careful time management to ensure it is a short pacey bell work activity and I advise avoiding making the content over-complicated otherwise it is difficult to review appropriately at the end of the lesson. It is, however, also an excellent activity when extended to a starter or a plenary.

Learning outcomes

Learning outcomes are one of the ways in which we engage pupils in learning. Sharing learning outcomes with pupils, for a lesson or series of lessons, is an important part of the learning process. Equally they form an essential part of the planning process. We can't plan for learning if we are not clear on the learning outcomes that we want pupils to achieve and pupils cannot gauge their achievement if they are not clear on what a successful outcome is. Combined with our planning, it is important to recognise that if pupils can see the bigger picture, and identify how they are going to get there (the next steps in their learning), then they will engage better with the learning process. Specific criteria (graded or not) offer something by which pupils can measure their success or progress. They are an essential component of assessment during learning and are used to inform differentiation. There are lots of different terms used: learning outcomes, learning intentions, learning objectives, learning successes and, whichever your school chooses to use (although there are subtle differences in the formal meaning of each), the important point is their use as part of the formative process. Simply displaying outcomes on a board and expecting pupils to absorb them is not enough. We need them to support the pupil in envisaging success. From this point we refer simply to learning outcomes.

Learning outcomes are best not directly differentiated as this leads to multiple learning outcomes, each with three or more success criteria, resulting in a confused learning environment. Best practice is for there to be one over-arching learning outcome and a clear list of success criteria. Success criteria offer natural differentiation and act as a progress ladder in learning, which pupils can use to measure their progress and demonstrate an increase in conceptual development.

How you phrase learning outcomes and success criteria and the language that you use is extremely important. Very often pupils are exposed to statements paraphrased in 'pupil speak' and caution must be taken if you do this, mainly because one of the problems as pupils progress through school is that they do not use subject-specific language comfortably and if we avoid this in the early years then we will never develop learners that can compete in the international market. However, it is important that pupils can access and understand learning outcomes and success criteria. My advice is to use the correct terminology (don't simply copy objectives direct from a curriculum or standards model written for teachers) in a clear and concise way and discuss the meaning openly with pupils. Make sure the learning outcome connects to the learning in the lesson and that the success criteria allow pupils to easily assess whether they have achieved the learning outcome (if pupils cannot decipher the meaning of a learning outcome or success criteria then they will not use them as part of the learning process). I advise using Bloom's Taxonomy when writing learning outcomes (Bloom and Krathwohl, 1956), choosing verbs like evaluate, compare, solve, construct, classify, develop, examine, predict, formulate, justify, rather than 'I will know how to' or 'I will understand how to'. The website http://teaching.uncc.edu/articles-books/best-practice-articles/goals-objectives/writing-objectives-using-blooms-taxonomy has examples of verbs and questions that use Bloom's Taxonomy and can help support the writing of learning outcomes, allowing you to differentiate success criteria through development of thinking skills (focusing on learning) rather than a to-do list of objectives (focusing on doing or the accomplishment of tasks). It is also important to develop subject literacy and so ensure that you include key words or phrases and that pupils are encouraged to use these during the lesson.

Teachers often use three success criteria and I think this has historical roots in the 'all, most, some' approach to learning. They also often assign grades to success criteria. I must address both of these issues here and state clearly that, in my opinion, the use of both 'all, most, some' and grades limits progress. The first point is perhaps mostly to do with the mind-set of pupils. Unfortunately, in some cases, pupils who only ever achieve the 'all' criteria, when it comes to subsequent lessons, only ever expect to achieve the 'all' criteria and don't look beyond this. Consciously or not they limit their own progress. Some pupils (who perhaps may not be highly motivated learners) may stop at the 'most', thinking that they have done 'just enough'. They won't attempt to address the 'some' because they don't challenge themselves. This therefore limits learning. Thus, labelling outcomes in this way can result in lowering pupils' expected progress. Progressive success criteria are much more open to all pupils achieving as there is no expectation for pupils to be in a particular learning category and allows for better assessment during the learning process. You can vary the number of progressive criteria, three in one lesson or perhaps five may be more appropriate in another. Sometimes these are referred to as learning ladders and they follow the natural progression of learning in the lesson – in other words the starter may focus on the first progress marker, the following activity the next and so on. There is the opportunity for these progression markers or success criteria themselves to be differentiated by development at different depths, although I would avoid sub-success criteria and simply approach this through differentiated learning materials. If we make things too busy we disengage from the outset as pupils see 'too much' as being unachievable. Grading of success criteria is also controversial and I would avoid assigning direct grades. First the grading system is supposed to reflect a generalised ability in the subject and is not specific to one particular criteria (although experience tells us if achievement in a particular topic is indicative of grade A or grade E for example). Second, grading can be demoralising. For those who are high-achieving it is fantastic, but for those who see they are only working towards a grade F it can be somewhat demoralising and have an adverse effect on some of these pupils who then 'don't see the point' of working in that particular subject as they won't achieve, for example, a grade C. Therefore I would avoid specific grades and discuss generalised achievement if necessary. Success criteria should be accessible for all pupils but how pupils achieve the success criteria may be at different levels or by using different support mechanisms. For example, if the success criterion was to expand two brackets of the form $(ax+b)(cx+d)$ then this may be differentiated, not explicitly in the success criteria, but during the lesson, depending upon pupil outcomes from a mini-assessment. Some pupils may confidently approach any problem of this form and others may require prompts and scaffolding (such as a number grid) or might only be confident with positive integers. If we were to list all of the possible outcome scenarios then pupils would be exposed to a long check list of sub-criteria for each success criteria in the lesson, which makes it difficult to focus learning. Much better is to ask pupils to think about how they have met the success criteria and any areas they need to develop further to fully secure it.

Instead of discussing learning outcomes and listing success criteria at the start of the lesson, some teachers (often those in more creative subjects or during discovery-based learning) prefer to allocate a few minutes as the lesson develops to ask pupils to decide on what the learning outcomes for the lesson might be/have been, and what the success criteria are/would be in identifying progress and how they can take the next steps in developing learning, giving pupils only a title at the beginning of the lesson. This is a nice activity as it encourages pupils to really think about what they have learnt and how they know they were successful in learning it. It also allows for pupils to differentiate their own outcomes and success criteria and focus on areas for development.

Some teachers also like to decontextualise learning outcomes believing that this supports pupils in transferring the underlying skill to different contexts. So, for example, with the muddled learning objective 'to write a newspaper report about the Great Fire of London' pupils will focus more on the Great Fire of London (the context) rather than the skill (formative writing). If we make the learning objective 'to write a newspaper article' and separate the context 'about the Great Fire of London' then pupils can more easily separate the skill from the context and are therefore more likely to be able to transfer the skill itself to any context (Clarke, 2008). This means they assess their progress against two measures: the content (knowledge of the Great Fire of London) and the ability to write a formative article. Success criteria can be assigned to both aspects and this allows you to differentiate.

Examples of learning outcomes with possible success criteria are given below (some taken from Bartlett, 2015). Note that there is no need for pupils to write learning outcomes or success criteria down as this simply wastes valuable learning time. If you want pupils to have a copy of the learning outcomes or accompanying criteria then print them off for pupils to refer to during the lesson. The learning outcome is generic and offers a general theme for the lesson, and the success criteria act as progress checkers (or progress ladders) and so, in many ways, it is useful for pupils to be able to have access to these at all times to enable them to assess their own progress (remember different pupils may be accessing different success criteria at different stages in the lesson).

Learning outcome: I will investigate and develop a method to expand and simplify the product of two linear brackets and apply these skills to different problems.

Success Criteria: as I work towards the learning outcome I will be able to:

- multiply a single term over a bracket, for example $3(a+2)$;
- develop a method to expand and simplify the product of two simple linear brackets, for example $(x-1)(x+2)$, explaining how I have done this;
- apply this method to expand an expression such as $(3x+5)(2x+3)$ or $(a-p)(2p+q)$ and be confident in explaining to others how I have done this;
- explain which method I use, and why, when solving different problems.

This example can be used to highlight that success criteria may be achieved at different levels. Taking the first 'multiply a single term over a bracket, for example $3(a+2)$', some pupils may only be able to cope with questions where a is a positive integer. Others will be confident tackling questions such as $-5(3-6b)$. If we had only had a success criterion that covered the latter then the less able would not be able to achieve this criteria. We also don't want to have so many success criteria that it becomes unmanageable by listing all possibilities. The other way to approach this is to have general criteria such as $a(bx+c)$ and we ask pupils to give examples of how they have achieved the specific criteria and any areas of development.

Learning outcome: I will investigate how the greatest female monarchs compare justifying my decisions.

Success criteria: as I work towards the learning outcome I will be able to:

* identify the key elements of Elizabeth I, Victoria and Elizabeth II's reign;
* determine criteria or categories for a monarch's success;
* analyse and compare each monarch's success;
* justify who I think was the best monarch.

Again, with these success criteria pupils will explore each at different depths, depending on their ability, and should be able to evidence these.

Learning outcome: I will be able to discuss how considered vocabulary choices create a range of effects in writing about superheroes.

Success criteria: as I work towards the learning outcome I will be able to:

* identify vocabulary choices and discuss how meaning is created through our choice of words;
* understand how writers structure different texts and why;
* analyse extracts from novels and graphic novels and compare their impact and justify and discuss different interpretations;
* create a short story in two different forms.

Learning outcomes: I will be able to recognise and understand that the world has many different natural regions.

Success criteria: as I work towards the learning outcome I will be able to:

* identify the world's major biomes and highlight them on a map;
* describe, in detail, where each of these biomes are located (referring to direction/ latitude data);
* discuss the factors that define eco-systems;
* discuss and compare biome characteristics.

Learning outcomes and success criteria are an extremely important part of the learning process and, however you refer to them (outcomes, objectives, intentions, etc.), it is essential that they are used regularly to support learning in lessons. Remember that not only do they allow pupils and teachers to measure pupil progress, they also allow you to plan lessons effectively. If you know what you want pupils to achieve then you can differentiate activities that allow all learners in the class the opportunity to access learning and to make progress. This is the art of an outstanding lesson.

The Big Question

A Big Question is a question that we ask all pupils at some point during the beginning of the lesson. It is used as a comparative assessment tool, providing tangible evidence of progress, and is typically a question that asks pupils to apply their learning. Pupils answer the question at the start of the lesson (spend only a couple of minutes on this) and return to it at the end of the lesson where they re-attempt the question. You can make it quite fun by asking pupils to keep their answer top secret by sealing it in an envelope. At the end of the lesson, when they have re-attempted the question, they can open their envelope to compare answers (pupils like the envelope strategy as it highlights the importance of the activity and is something a little different). Hopefully pupils have made substantial progress both in terms of formulating a response and in their use of subject specific language and terminology identifying where and how they have made progress. The power of the activity being in pupils comparing their initial and final response. The question itself, when posed direct to all pupils, is not differentiated as pupils are all asked the same question. It is the pupil outcomes that then determine different levels of progress. Having said that, you may give some pupils the opportunity to use prompts or have hint cards prepared to support their final response (we discuss this in Chapter 5) and allow pupils to self-select whether they need a resource to support their answer. While not explicitly differentiated in this way we can differentiate the Big Question by personalising it, giving each pupil a question in an envelope that you want them to be able to answer at the end of the lesson. Be careful about making the questions too varied as this limits the opportunity for whole class discussion at the end of the lesson. If you do this then it is best to use the responses in individual reflection time and you can check this when you mark work. Alternatively, use this as a group activity and give different groups different Big Questions, thus differentiating by grouping and also by task. You can present comparative activities in lots of different ways and there are many variations. For example, a similar activity is to ask pupils to note down at the start of the lesson three things that they already know about the topic they are going to study and/or three things they would like to find out. At the end of the lesson they can determine whether their learning has developed sufficiently in order for them to now address these points.

Whichever approach you take one of the key techniques is to get pupils to analyse their responses – why did they initially approach the question as they did? What have they developed in the lesson that means they now take a different approach? What misconceptions did they have at the start of the lesson? How do they know? What aspects do they need to improve on further? Has the Big Question highlighted areas for development? This develops metacognitive skills, encouraging pupils to really think about the learning, and is far more powerful than asking pupils to summarise the over-used question in our classrooms 'what have I learnt today?' We all know from experience that asking pupils to answer this question simply leads to them regurgitating learning outcomes and, in reality, in doing this they don't think about thinking, they simply carry out a very basic process. In 'doing' the comparison activity (Big

Question or otherwise) pupils are much more likely to retain information, it shows them clearly what they have learnt in the lesson, and they are much more likely to be able to articulate this progress in learning, explain how they know they have met the learning outcomes/success criteria for the lesson and identify any areas that they need to develop. Their initial and final responses can be stuck into their books as evidence of their progress and success in learning. Remember progress is progress, it just might be at different rates for different individuals. All pupils should feel positive about learning and this activity supports this process by allowing them to visibly see their personal achievement, and we should celebrate all success (however small).

The activities so far are short: a couple of minutes for bell work, a minute or so for introducing the learning outcomes (don't spend too long going through each success criteria with pupils – they only need a flavour at the start of the lesson – because learning outcomes and success criteria are workable statements which, by their nature, are to be returned to regularly throughout the lesson to allow pupils to assess their own progress), and two minutes for the Big Question. Maintaining the pace of the lesson is very important to drive learning. We are a maximum of five or six minutes in at this stage.

Examples of Big Questions (Bartlett, 2015):

1) Can a flame change colour? (Obviously initially this would be a yes/no response or pupils may attempt an answer – but at the end of the lesson you would expect pupils to explain and offer examples – pupil responses are given in Chapter 5.)

2) How does an aeroplane stay in the sky? (Obviously initially you will get a variety of responses or guesses and some may be based on scientific hypotheses – but at the end of the lesson you would expect pupils to be able to explain why, to use examples and to use key words.)

3) What is the area of a rectangle with width $(a + 2)$ and length $(4a + 3)$? (Responses to this Big Question are shown in Chapter 5.)

4) Do these numbers belong in the same sequence?
   2, 5, 8, 11, 14, …
   …, 299, 302, 305, 308, ….

5) Do plants need light? (Pupil responses to this Big Question are shown in Chapter 5.)

6) Do polar bears like the cold?

7) When the ice melts the level of the water will stay the same/rise/fall? (By the end of the lesson you would expect pupils to be able to justify their choice with scientific explanation.)

8) Where would you choose to go on holiday: Australia or Belize? (Put up pictures – comparing two destinations. A good Big Question which focuses on tourism.)

9) Why are many of my clothes made outside of the UK?

10) Why do we call some religions 'mythologies' (ancient Greek, Norse, Egyptian, etc.) and others religions?

11) How would we find out how much salt there is in the ocean?

12) What is true strength?

13) Is it easier to be Queen in the twenty-first century?

14) Why does this bar of steel sink and steel boats float? (As with the aeroplane question, we would expect use of scientific language and a focus on the 'why' by the end of the lesson.)

15) If I flick the switch will the light bulb light? (A good Big Question for lessons on circuits in physics.)

16) What happens next...? (For example, in the mixing of two chemicals – we are asking pupils to make a prediction and when they return to the question at the end of the lesson they have to decide whether their prediction was correct, or correct any misconceptions and create a new prediction focusing on the 'why' and the 'why not'.)

17) Can we always go back to where we started from? (In the context of reversible and irreversible chemical reactions.)

18) Which came first...? (Useful in lots of different contexts.)

19) How much does a cloud weigh? (A rather abstract question but points to scientific method and is current topical research in the UK.)

20) Is water from the Gulf of Mexico responsible for the mild climate in Britain?

21) Questions that involve a misconception and asking pupils to agree or disagree are good Big Questions as pupils must unpick an error, thus demonstrating a good understanding. For example, Kate says 'it will either rain or not rain so the probability that it will rain tomorrow is 50 per cent' or the advert says '8 out of 10 cats prefer Whiskas'. Annie says 'I have 5 cats, so does this mean 4 of them would prefer to eat Whiskas cat food?'

22) 'When am I ever going to use...in real life?' or '...is the reason why we...' or 'do you think...is responsible for...'. This always proves interesting. At the start of the lesson you will probably get responses such as 'never' or 'no idea', but at the end of the lesson pupils should be able to draw from their learning and think about different applications of the topic.

The first learning cycle: the starter activity

The first learning cycle in the lesson is often referred to as the starter activity and it acts as the learning hook. It usually has a different purpose to the learning cycle or cycles in the main part of the lesson and/or plenary as it is commonly used to benchmark – to know where pupils are starting from (often assessing a point of knowledge). This information is then used as a basis for differentiation as the lesson progresses or to make a connection with learning from a recent lesson. A more open starter will, for example, begin an investigation or rich task (possibly linked to new learning opportunities). The structure of the learning cycle may therefore be different to that in the main body of the lesson. It begins the learning journey and so needs to gain the interest of pupils. For that reason it needs to be well planned, pitched at the right level, offer a degree of challenge, allow you to make an assessment and link to the learning in the lesson. Pace is essential and it is important not to allow the starter activity to drift. If this happens before you know it 20 minutes of the lesson are lost, along with the interest of the class. It is also necessary to ensure that learners can access the activity (pre-planned differentiation) and achieve some success (otherwise they disengage and think the lesson is going to be 'too hard' for them). I recommend approximately 10 to 20 per cent of lesson time is allocated to the starter activity including review.

There are lots and lots of different styles of starter activity – outstanding teachers will use a variety of approaches. Irrespective of the activity itself, the most important part is what you do with it. Assessment and review form an essential part of this process, informing future learning and differentiated pathways. So when you plan an activity, ask yourself the following:

- Am I and pupils clear on the learning purpose?
- Does the activity provide accurate benchmarking information – where pupils are starting from?
- Is it a useful activity on which to build?
- How does it work towards achieving the learning outcomes?
- What skills does it rely on or develop?
- How does it support development in the learning journey?
- Has it started to lay the foundations?
- Does it challenge all pupils at an appropriate level?
- Is it differentiated or does it provide sufficient information for subsequent differentiation?
- What is the quality of this information?
- Is it an open or closed starter activity?
- Does it allow pupils to assess which pathway they may need to take in the main body of the lesson?
- Can all pupils access the activity?

Asking these questions will help to ensure that progress is made and help you to support subsequent learning during the lesson. Position yourself in the place of the learner and imagine the outcomes you would expect to achieve from each activity and how they develop progress towards achieving the learning outcomes or success criteria for the lesson. Does it provide all of the information that you and they need to make an informed judgement on their progress? Now think about one of the most important questions, whether you can access the activity. If you were pupil X would you need any additional support? Can the same question be presented in different ways or use a different medium to support different learning needs and optimise outcomes for pupils? In the following section we look at starter activities that benchmark learning.

Benchmarking learning

When we benchmark learning we do so in order to determine what pupils already know and this acts as a platform for learning. If it demonstrates gaps in prior knowledge then these must be addressed before progressing. There are different ways to differentiate this type of activity; through direct differentiation of the activity itself or by using the activity to inform future differentiation. Typically, teachers benchmark knowledge at the start of a new topic rather than part way through a series of linked lessons and it usually consists of an activity that all pupils complete. This is to ascertain the level at which pupils are currently at and any gaps in knowledge that need to be closed. Of course the same questions can be given to pupils through a different medium and this in itself is a form of differentiation. For example, some pupils may be given words and others images; irrespective of how the activity is structured, it should really make pupils think. One of the most important factors identified by Ausubel *et al.* (1978) as influencing learning is what the learner already knows and then using this to inform practice. 'The most important single factor influencing learning is what the learner already knows. Ascertain this and teach him accordingly' (Ausubel *et al.*, 1978).

Quick-fire questions

Quick-fire questions are closed activities and are commonly used in classrooms to benchmark learning. They are not typically differentiated as the purpose is to ask all pupils the same question in order to assess starting points. Some teachers do, however, offer supporting information, which is itself a form of differentiation (similar to scaffolding). For example, those pupils who are known to struggle with their times-tables may be given a multiplication grid so that the focus of the exercise in the mathematics example below is whether they understand the process of multiplying terms over brackets rather than whether they can recall their multiplication tables (although obviously there is a focus on the importance of learning these). The success criteria of expanding expressions and simplifying terms may then be met, whereas without the supporting grid a pupil who has limited recall of times-tables may not have been able to access the work as they would have been lost with the pace of the questioning (spending far too long trying to work out their times-tables) and would potentially be disengaged from the outset. Accessibility is integral to differentiation. Always think about the key factors that may limit access to an activity and, if these are secondary to the primary purpose of the activity, then devise strategies or materials to support the secondary process in order for all pupils to be able to achieve the primary goal.

Expand the following expressions and simplify where appropriate:

1) $3(a+2)$
2) $4(b-7)$
3) $-6(2a+1)$
4) $-8(7-2m)$
5) $3(5p+4) - 7(2p-1)$
6) $y(2y-3) + 2y(3y+2)$

To emphasise the comments made earlier relating to this example, the primary purpose is whether pupils understand how to multiply terms over brackets and understand the mathematical statements. If access is limited by being unable, for example, to multiply -8×7 (Question 4) then they will not be focusing on the underlying concept and will get 'muddled' and fall behind. Supporting the learning with a multiplication grid allows them to access the primary purpose. They can work on their times-tables at home or in additional numeracy support classes.

In this type of activity the answer is either correct or incorrect. However, some short response questions are suited to quick-fire benchmarking activities. These are questions where there is the possibility of more than one answer but that do not lead to lengthy debate or discussion. For example, if we were asking pupils to describe an image of Labrador puppy with one adjective they may say 'cute', 'cuddly', 'golden' and so on. None of these answers are wrong and differentiation occurs through the level of language. In English we might ask pupils to write down key quotations or characters from Romeo and Juliet beginning with each letter of the word Romeo, or to find phrases in Shakespeare's works that we use in modern-day English such as, for example, 'the green-eyed monster' (Othello). Differentiation is then by outcome but can also be through support during the activity. For example, for those pupils who may need further guidance, you might already have prepared a series of quotes on a sheet of A4 from which they pick the best quote or match quotes and meanings. This supports learning but, at the same time, allows all pupils to access the activity (albeit at differing levels of challenge) and to make progress. All pupils can then contribute to the subsequent discussion – allowing for meaningful review.

Making the most of quick-fire questions is important and accurate assessment of pupils' answers typically comes through your use of targeted questioning. It is this assessment that determines future learning pathways (differentiated routes). If the assessment is not high quality then simply using a quantitative score to allocate pupils to different learning pathways (perhaps different levels of work) is pointless. A numerical score does not tell you the level of a pupil's understanding of the underlying concepts and is simply a superficial indicator. A pupil who can simply regurgitate a method without understanding is very different from a pupil who has a deep understanding of a concept, yet both pupils may produce the same (correct) answer to a quick-fire question; always use questioning to probe learning and to determine the depth of understanding. I also recommend layering questions and making sure that you do not simply ask, for example, ten identical questions. It is important if you are benchmarking knowledge to ask progressively challenging questions that each identify particular aspects in learning or specific skills. This gives insight into particular learning needs where you may differentiate resources.

Quick-fire questions can be answered by pupils on mini-whiteboards (use the word 'reveal' when you want pupils to hold up their boards to avoid copying) or individually in their books. If you use mini-whiteboards then questioning should follow each 'reveal', otherwise review each question at the end of the activity through basketball-style questioning, determining whether any underlying concepts are secure. We discuss questioning techniques in Chapter 7 and it is very important that questioning is used correctly to develop learning.

The 5Ws

The 5Ws is a starter activity that can be used across different subjects: who, what, when, where, why. It provides differentiation by outcome (they are open questions), although there is an argument that you can differentiate by task here and certainly by your use of targeted questioning. Often this is used as a preliminary activity as an opener to a research-based lesson. It might be that initially you watch a brief clip and ask pupils to note the 5Ws and this is used as a basis for evidence gathering and report writing as the lesson progresses. It can then be used in a developmental way. Do their 5Ws change as they gather evidence from different sources? Why have they changed? How do they know?

'Odd one out'

'Odd one out' activities can be used at all phases of the lesson, albeit with a slightly different emphasis (we previously discussed these activities as bell work where it is important to keep the exercise simple and something pupils can 'do' unaided). They can be basic activities or extremely challenging and can involve simple recall or higher-order thinking skills. The same context can be used but at different levels of challenge and cognitive demand – this makes it an ideal activity for differentiating learning. The purpose as an activity is to go beyond simple identification and to encourage pupils to think about the 'why' and the 'why not' (focusing on classification and justification). However, remember that if used for bell work (as previously discussed) we need to be brief and so, used in this context, it is best to stick to recall with discussion during reverse bell work at the end of the lesson. A simple template is shown in Figure 3.1. It can be used for all levels and all subjects and need not be over-complicated (it is the resulting discussion that challenges thinking). It may involve words, statements, images, key terms and so on (or a mixture of some or all of these). It can be tailored to the individual by issuing different 'odd one out' cards and this may be something you chose to do as bell work if different pupils need different subject areas to be reinforced.

Examples from different subjects to demonstrate the breadth of this activity are listed below for similar topics.

- Biology (cells, organs and systems):
  - Cell membrane, nucleus, mitochondria, glycogen granules;
  - Connective, blood, muscle, reproductive;
  - Small intestine, kidney, pancreas, stomach;
  - Thyroid, pituitary gland, pancreas, liver.

- Art:
  - ○ Azure, sapphire, cerulean, blue;
  - ○ Impressionism, Monet, Matisse, Dali.
- DT:
  - ○ Plywood, MDF, pine, chipboard;
  - ○ Pencil, china-graph pencil, chisel, scriber.

There are lots of variations of 'odd one out' and this type of activity simply consolidates prior learning and allows you to assess learning and differentiate through targeted questioning. Without assessing the activity, it is meaningless and loses its power (discussed in Chapter 6). One way to develop this activity further is to ask pupils to add one word to a set that would still keep the odd one out the same. This provides natural differentiation and encourages pupils to really think about the context – i.e. it develops higher-order thinking skills. Another variation is to give pupils sets of words like, for example, a list of 20 words. They need to group words initially into groups of three (there will be some cards left – these are the 'odd one outs') and then select one of the remaining words as the odd one out (resulting in five sets of four words) – the focus here is on reasoning and you can obviously differentiate by giving pupils different sets. Some may be made more challenging by having words that are more closely associated and therefore careful thought and reasoning would be needed to classify them correctly.

Figure 3.1 An example of a template for the 'odd one out'.

Pair-matching activities

Pair-matching activities are probably one of the easiest activities to differentiate and are popular for this reason. They are also an excellent tool for learning. You can use definitions with differing degrees of complexity and tailor the resource according to pupils' learning needs. They are particularly useful in a series of lessons where recent prior learning can be used to allocate specific levels of challenge to pupils or groups of pupils. It doesn't limit learning, it enhances it, and if all pupils are using the resource in a similar way then whole class discussions do not become fragmented but can be developed with ease. Equally they can be used as a source at the beginning of a new topic to generate questions that pupils need to answer as the lesson progresses. In other words they complete the activity in a more open way and it is left as an activity that is not assessed in terms of the content at the beginning of the lesson but in terms of the quality of the questions pupils raise as a result, which they can return to at any point during the lesson to answer. We end up with a list of, for example, ten focused questions. The activity can then be assessed at an appropriate point in the lesson as learning develops – pupils may revisit it. Discussion surrounds any changes that pupils made and any newly acquired knowledge. An example of a simple pair-matching exercise is shown in Figure 3.2. Pupils are asked to find the matching expression. This can be adapted to different levels of challenge for different pupils (differentiating by task).

A further example of a matching exercise is shown in Figure 3.3 for vitamins. Pupils need to match the appropriate vitamin with its sources and what it is needed for. This can be differentiated by giving pupils all sources on one card so, for example, for Vitamin A place green and yellow vegetables and dairy products on one card (i.e. only one card to match), or adding challenge by putting the sources on different cards, leaving two cards to match to Vitamin A. This would give the opportunity to differentiate by pace.

$3(a + 2)$	$3a^2 + 3a$
$7(2a - 8)$	$-8a + 12$
$8(2a - 1)$	$-15a + 15$
$5(-3a + 3)$	$14a + 56$
$7(2a + 8)$	$16a - 8$
$-4(2a - 3)$	$3a + 6$
$3a(a + 1)$	$15a - 15$
$5(3a - 3)$	$14a - 56$
$-7(2a - 8)$	$-16a - 8$
$-8(2a + 1)$	$-14a + 56$

Figure 3.2 A pair-matching exercise where pupils are asked to match equivalent expressions.

Vitamin	Need for	Sources
Vitamin A	Good skin Healthy skin Growth	Green and yellow vegetables Dairy products
Vitamin B (thiamine, riboflavin, niacin)	Release energy from foods Healthy skin	Breads Milk Eggs
Vitamin B12	Red blood cells	Meat Milk Eggs
Vitamin C	Healthy skin Protects cells Helps absorb iron	Fruit Vegetables
Vitamin D	Helps absorb calcium Strong teeth and bones	Margarine Oily fish

Figure 3.3 An example of a pair-matching exercise where pupils are asked to match vitamins with their respective source and what they are needed for.

Pair–matching activities can be completed individually, in pairs or small groups, and are used to promote discussion between peers, i.e. they have to justify their choices to each other and the thinking and sharing underpins this activity. Tailoring your own resources is important if you are using differentiated learning strategies. There are lots of excellent sources of resource that can be used to generate pair-matching exercises on www.bbcbitesize.co.uk for all subjects and levels. It may be appropriate for you to leave one box blank for pupils (again tailor this) where they have to write the best definition. Pair-matching does not have to be a paper-based exercise. There are many online activities that can be used with an interactive white-board. It also doesn't have to be simply pair-matching with words. For example, in geography, when classifying types of rocks, you might have images of igneous, sedimentary and metamorphic rocks that pupils have to match with the correct definition. For some pupils you might extend the level of challenge by including different types within a classification, for example, basalt and granite (igneous rocks) or sandstone, limestone, clay and chalk (sedimentary rocks). This would add more depth to the exercise for a more-able pupil.

Pair-matching activities or resources can also be used in a 'find your partner' activity. Each pupil has a piece of laminated A4 card and they have to find their match. An alternative is 'making connections' where pupils have to find others with statements that have a connection to their statement resulting in pupils forming a little group with similar information. The obvious way to differentiate this activity is by the level of the information pupils are given (differentiation by ability) and by the groupings that they subsequently form. You must therefore give careful consideration to both to ensure that all pupils are challenged. You must give pupils thinking time before the 'mad dash' to find their partner (prepare yourself for lots of learning noise at this point) – perhaps give pupils a list of all statements to read in silence for two minutes in order to decide on their 'match' or 'matches', which they then have to find. This activity is usually well-received by all learners and in particular by those with a kinaesthetic preference that perhaps find standard written tasks more restrictive. Once pupils form their 'learning group' you may want to pose a further challenge or question for them to develop or return to as a group as the lesson progresses. This can also be differentiated.

Game-based activities

Traditional board games are commonly used in classrooms and examples include Battleships, Snakes and Ladders, Guess Who, Taboo and Bingo. While they are very different games they have one common use in the classroom with subject-specific questions in place of the traditional board-game questions. The way to ensure that this type of activity progresses learning is to be very clear on the learning purpose (both for you and for pupils), ensuring that you match the questions to the needs of the learners to secure outcomes. Pupils must feel that this is not simply something they are 'doing' (in other words passing the time until you say stop), but an activity that develops thinking skills and applies their learning, and so becoming an important component of the lesson. One way to differentiate is to use colour-coded question cards (for example, pink, purple, blue) of differing degrees of challenge (or perhaps topic). The colour pupils select can be based on prior assessment or through pupil choice by simply 'having a go' and encouraging self-selection. Alternatively, pupils can pick 'pink card 1' but if they struggle with that they then select 'purple card 1', which scaffolds the question or has a useful hint. If they need further support they select 'blue card 1' and finally a yellow 'ask a peer or a teacher' card. Pupils need to log which coloured card they used for each question and this will build up a useful assessment chart (or tracking grid) for both you and them to assess areas of strength and areas of development and how future learning may be differentiated (a learning profile). To support this process and ensure that pupils focus on learning (not simply game playing) it is useful to add a parallel task. This may be something as simple as: 'write down the question you found most challenging, focusing on why it challenged you and what information you would need to answer the question'. If pupils simply 'play the game' then the activity is pointless. Always think about what you want pupils to get out of an activity and then work backwards to design that activity to (hopefully) achieve these outcomes.

With an activity such as Bingo, which is usually a whole-class activity, it is difficult to differentiate the questions (because we ask everyone the same question). Therefore, this is an activity that I would potentially avoid and certainly avoid with a mixed-ability class. Why? Because while it may appear fun (often mistaken for engagement), if you target the 'middle'-ability pupils then pupils of lower ability will not be able to access the questions and learners of a higher ability will not be challenged enough. Both groups of pupil potentially disengage. Conversely, descriptive activities such as 'Taboo' or 'Who Am I?' are excellent as a differentiated resource. Taboo is a game where pupils have to describe a hidden word without using the word itself and their partner guesses what it is. 'Who (or what) am I?' relies on pupils asking questions to determine the person or item. You can obviously differentiate by giving pupils different words or people. One of the important aspects of this activity is that you then do something with it and ask pupils to write down, for example, the best dictionary definition of the term they had (Taboo) or three questions that would have enabled them to guess the person or object more quickly (in other words they then have to focus on key characteristics, which is higher-order thinking). You may have pre-prepared key points for each character that can be given to pupils later to assess against your criteria – were any points the same or similar? Were any points different? Why? This can form the basis of self-assessment. Would they now change any of their key points? If so why? Comparing their statements with yours really promotes thinking skills and self-assessment and if they choose to remain with their original set then how are these better? If they gave them to another pupil to guess who the character was – would they be able to? Alternatively, the class can pool their descriptive points and come up with a description of a particular character that remains visible (perhaps use a large piece of paper and stick on a wall) and, as the lesson or series of lessons progress and more text is studied, they can decide if they would develop, add to or change any of the statements. Does the individual character develop? Have other factors played a part? This description becomes dynamic and, at any point, pupils can go and add to the poster or, at key points, you can stop the learning and ask pupils if there is anything they would like to add or remove from the list. It almost becomes an interactive learning wall.

More open starters

Setting the scene through rich tasks or investigations creates a wonderful opportunity to have a more open-ended starter activity (we discuss investigative tasks in Chapter 4). Open-ended starters encourage pupils to develop their thinking and problem-solving skills. They can be individual or beat-the-clock team starters. Most importantly, they really engage pupils' subject thinking and their ability to apply their thinking. In business studies, for example, develop a brand by starting with a series of images and then asking pupils to collectively write their thoughts (individually, in pairs and then as a group – having no prior technical language or knowledge). This is not a closed starter and will naturally lead to an open discussion that acts as a precursor to the activities for developing a brand and a unique selling point. In science there are also some useful examples based around forensic science discovery lessons. Websites such as www.theguardian.com/teacher-network/teacher-blog/2013/mar/27/forensic-science-csi-teaching-tips-classroom have some excellent ideas.

Another example of this type of activity are statement starters where pupils are asked to make an initial choice based on the statement or evidence presented to them. For example, in a citizenship lesson place these statements on differently coloured A4 paper:

> I believe that responsibilities are more important than rights. Citizenship should emphasise the social role of the citizen far more than the individual's rights.

Rights on their own lead to selfishness and irresponsibility. Shared goals and the life of the community are more important than individual self-interest. (Statement A.)

I believe that rights are more important than responsibilities. The state is a necessary evil that restricts my ability to act as I wish. The emphasis in citizenship should be on protecting my individual rights. This will allow me to act independently and pursue my own interests. The only responsibility I have to the community is to protect these rights and the rights of others. (Statement B.)

I believe that rights and responsibilities shouldn't be in opposition to each other, but are dependent on each other. We are all individuals but we are also rooted in the community. Through participation in the community we both protect our rights and promote social justice. (Statement C.)

Produce a larger A3 poster of each statement (try to keep this the same colour as the corresponding A4 sheets given to pupils, or label them clearly) and stick them on the wall in different corners of the room. When you give the signal pupils write down their choice in secret (to avoid them changing it when they see where their friends go). When told to do so they must then go and stand by the statement they agree with. This leads to the learning discussion – pupils justifying their choice. Keep a note on timings (you don't want this discussion to dominate or to drift) and ask a pupil from each group to summarise in 30 seconds the key points from their corner. Once these have been heard, give pupils 20 seconds thinking time to decide whether, having heard the different arguments, they want to change their initial choice and move to another group (again this can be noted in secret to avoid 'friendship' moves). Those who move then have to justify their decision and those who remain have to justify their decision. Differentiation here is through the use of questioning. Another take on this activity is to ask pupils which statement best describes different scenarios, for example, at their school, in the local community, etc. The aim of the final discussion is to determine three questions that would help them to decide which statement they think is correct: Do they need more information? What information do they need? Does it depend on the context? What context are the quotes written in? Once the three key questions are selected these can be used as a basis for future assessment (the quality of these questions allows you to assess the level of learning). Differentiation is by outcome and the quality of the discussions and the concluding three key questions demonstrate the extent to which pupils have synthesised the information.

Grid starters such as, for example, in geography where you might use masking tape to create a grid on the floor of the classroom, are also open activities. In this activity, place objects in the grid (or ask pupils to). Pupils then have to identify where specific objects are using grid coordinates like, for example, A4 or B3. Is this sufficient to pinpoint the exact location? Photograph an object (this can be linked to the projector and displayed at the point of comparison) and then remove the object. Ask a pupil to place it in, for example, A3 – is it in precisely the same place as it was before? Alternatively put another object in the same square and ask pupils for its location (A3). This will enable pupils to visualise that simply knowing A3 as a coordinate, for example, does not pinpoint the exact location – it gives us a region in which the object is located but it is not precise. This can lead to pupils discussing in groups how they might pinpoint the exact location. Your role is to circulate – asking probing questions to direct learning – and then to close the activity with a whole-class discussion resulting in a formal definition of grid coordinates. The lesson then progresses with pupils applying the skills they have developed in the starter activity building on their learning. In order to differentiate this type of activity you would perhaps use different grid structures or use them in different contexts relying on the application of skills.

Target boards

Target board starters provide natural differentiation. They involve having a grid on the board on which you base a series of questions. As you point to a square on the grid (which may contain a number, image, word or statement) pupils have to hold up their solution (this allows for whole class assessment and you can select a few responses for interesting discussions) or, alternatively, you ask a question and pupils have to select an answer from the grid. You can ask a variety of general questions, which reinforce vocabulary, understanding of concepts and mental strategies. This type of activity can be used across all subjects.

For example, in Table 3.1, questions might be of the form:

*   Can you identify a prime number? How do you know?
*   Can you identify a multiple of 4?
*   Which row has the greatest total?
*   Which numbers are square numbers? How do you know?
*   What is the square root of 36?

An alternative use is to tell pupils $a=4$, $b=-2$, $c=7$ and then point to a number on the grid and pupils have to hold up their answer. For example, if you point to -6 some pupils might write $a-b$ or $3b$ or $b+b+b$, etc. You can then talk about equivalent expressions, simplifying expressions, etc. You can adjust the level of difficulty to suit the group so, for example, you may use negative numbers such as $a=-3$, $b=5$, $c=-2$. This type of activity allows for natural differentiation by outcome.

Table 3.1 Target board grid.

-6	-4	19
1	2	6
32	49	-7

In languages this type of activity can be used with images. For example, you may have a grid with images of different animals on and read statements such as *cet animal aime manger des bananes*. Pupils then identify the animal (or letter if they cannot recall the animal's name). You may then ask pupils to write down one adjective that can be used to describe the animal or to write down a sentence describing the animal (differentiation according to their ability in the target language). An alternative is to ask pupils to sketch an image you describe (leave one grid square blank) based solely on the statement you read. You can glance at them and choose a couple for discussion (it often adds a bit of fun to the lesson). Another suggestion is that you point to an item in a square on the grid and ask pupils to write down the question (while this can be used as a starter activity this particular reverse use of the target board is perhaps better as a plenary as discussed in Chapter 5).

What's the connection?

This type of starter activity is typically differentiated by task. The idea being that pupils are given two concepts and they have to identify the connection between them. More-able pupils can be given concepts that are further apart or, alternatively, pupils can be given the same concepts but those who require more support can be given a hint card with a bridging connection. Examples from business studies include:

- Lean Production and Cash Flow?
- Acid Test and Bank Loan?

An alternative to this is sequencing. This is where pupils have to place images, words, phrases and so on in the correct order. In music this might include the opening section of the score of a familiar tune that is then cut up into bars. Pupils have to place them in the correct order to form the piece – drawing on their ability to read music. This can be done using resources such as musical instruments to support learners if needed (differentiation by resource). In a mixed ability group it may be appropriate to give individuals or groups of similar-ability pupils different pieces of music. In chemistry this can be adapted as a sequence of processes in an experiment. Pupils place them in the correct order. Indeed anything that we use in our lessons that requires things to be done in a given order can be translated with ease into this type of activity.

Dominoes is a game-based version. Dominoes can be created on card with terms, phrases, words and so on between which there is a connection. Pupils need to be able to understand in order to make the association. In MFL this could, for example, be matching the name of an animal and its description. It is similar to pair matching but can be extended to making connections between one or more term. Other variations include antonyms. Pupils can be given different levels, starting with something simple such as: black and white, fast and…. This can be used when developing language skills, testing pupil's understanding of a word or when introducing a new word.

50

Video technology

Using technology in learning is excellent for engaging some groups of learners. Differentiation can be through use of technology as a resource (some pupils watch a video clip for example) or with all pupils using the technology but at different ability levels. A useful tool is for pupils to watch a clip (use headphones) and then extract information (based on questions you provide). Pupils can be asked the same or different questions and they then come together to form discussion groups or as a whole class. The idea being that you can tailor this activity to the individual. In MFL, for example, pupils might listen to an audio but be expected to answer questions at different levels of challenge depending on their proficiency in the target language. This might extend to a 'what comes next…' scenario. Alternatively, pupils might listen to different audio resources at different levels of ability. These approaches all differentiate the learning experience.

Objects

The use of objects enhances learning like, for example, using a potato in business studies. Pupils are asked in teams to base a business around the potato (the obvious ones are 'chips' or 'crisps') and they then have to develop a brand, marketing, packaging and so on, as the series of lessons progresses. In geography bring in a set of rocks (possibly from a field trip): 'What is it? Where is it from?' This might be linked to coastal erosion – pupils write down three things they already know about coastal erosion in two minutes on a post-it note and post it on the learning board. You can carefully select a few post-it notes for discussion and highlight any misconceptions as these are important in the learning process. An alternative example from drama could be where pupils are given an image and they have to act it. This forms a basis for discussion (again with no right or wrong answer) and then, as aspects of drama are developed during the lesson, they return to the image – does their representation now change? What have they done differently? How do they know? What impact does it have? This is a comparative exercise and allows pupils to review the different techniques that they have developed during the lesson. Differentiation here is by outcome, by grouping, by task or resource. In languages or English 'here's the image' are popular: what would the caption be? Who do you think it's for? Audience/purpose? This can be returned to at the end of the lesson to see if pupils' thinking has developed and pupils can use peer assessment to discuss their thoughts.

Targeted questioning

Targeted questioning is often used as a starter and questioning as a tool is excellent for differentiation. Often teachers throw a cuddly toy around as they ask questions (particularly with younger years), throwing it to the pupil who is to answer, and this is something that pupils seem to enjoy and can be used to increase the pace. To ensure that all pupils pay full attention and are thinking about the question that you ask, don't throw the toy until a few seconds after you pose the question. This keeps all pupils on their toes and allows for thinking time (count to three or four). If the lesson continues the learning theme from the previous lesson or lessons then use this technique to summarise prior learning rather than an exercise in a book. What did we learn last lesson? How do we know? Give me an example? Argue the case that...? Kate says '...' is she correct? Take care when throwing the 'cuddly toy' (health and safety). Chapter 7 discusses differentiation through questioning in detail.

Envelope activities

Sealed envelope tasks are popular with pupils and are particularly good for kinaes-thetic learners as they are actively 'doing' while thinking. They can be individual, paired or group tasks. Examples include statements or exercises that pupils have to complete to demonstrate learning, such as statement matching or sequencing exer-cises. You can differentiate tasks in this way, giving different pupils or groups dif-ferent activities in their envelopes. In a more autonomous learning environment encourage pupils to self-select based on their prior learning. If you have chosen to differentiate the activity, don't go over everything in the review – pupils will easily become disengaged. Instead, select a few questions that illustrate key points and use these for the basis of discussion to reinforce underlying concepts or processes. Figure 3.4 shows an example from PE where pupils are asked to match the muscle to its function and to an example in sport. To add further challenge leave some cards out so that pupils have to fill them in themselves (you may choose to differentiate by leaving out different cards for different pupils). In languages, for example, this type of activity can include new vocabulary and the corresponding definition (also useful in

Triceps	Extend the arm at the elbow	Press-ups, javelin
Biceps	Flex the arm at the elbow	Pull-up, drawing a bow in archery
Deltoids	Move the arm in all directions at the shoulder	Bowling a cricket ball
Pectorals	Adduct the arm at the shoulder	Forehand drive in tennis
Trapezius	Hold the shoulders in place, move the head back and sideways	Holding head up in rugby scrum
Quadriceps	Extend the leg at the knee	Kicking a ball jumping upwards
Hamstrings	Flex the leg at the knee	Bending knee before kicking a ball
Gastrocnemius	Pointing the toes, help to flex the knee	Running
Latissimus dorsi	Adduct and extend the arm at the shoulder	Butterfly stroke in swimming
Abdominals	Flex the trunk across the stomach	Pulling the body down when hurdling

Figure 3.4 Match the name of the muscle to its function, give an example in sport and then place these in the correct location on the diagram of the human body.

Rene Laennec	France	1816	Invented the stethoscope and started the practice of 'auscultation'.
Pierre Louis	France	1834	Argued that symptoms were irrelevant and that what was happening inside the body was much more important when it came to diagnosing illness. As a result, doctors made diagnoses on the basis of a full clinical examination of the 'signs' made by the disease on the body.
Carl Ruge	Germany	1878	Developed the technique of biopsy.
Carl Ludwig	Germany	1847	Invented the kymograph.
Wilhelm Roentgen	Germany	1895	Discovered x-rays.
Willem Einthoven	Holland	1900	Invented the electrocardiograph.

Figure 3.5 An example of a matching exercise taken from the history of medicine.

literacy at KS2). It can also be used for revision purposes, as illustrated in Figure 3.5 in this History activity on nineteenth-century methods of diagnosis and treatment. Cut all of the sections into cards and place them in an envelope. Pupils can then match the correct terms.

These activities can also be used as a basis for 'find your match'. This allows you to form new focus groups who work together for the remainder of the lesson, enabling you to carefully select the working group and thus differentiate by grouping and then by activity or task (ability-based).

Review starters

Activities that involve pupils reviewing material are open-ended and in order to achieve the maximum benefit in a short time some pupils will need guidance. The purpose is that pupils write a response either individually, in pairs or in groups. The key to making this successful is to ask pupils to do something specific, such as to write down three key points, or to write down two key questions, or to write down two things they liked and one thing that they would do to improve. They must then justify their decision to another pair.

Other activities include comparison exercises such as voting on two different podcasts, on two different solutions to a problem or on alternative articles. These type of activities encourage pupils to think. This can easily be differentiated by giving pupils different sources as the focus is on both the skill and subject content. Which is the best and why? As the lesson and learning develops does their decision change? Why? This is a useful starter if you are going to ask pupils to develop a podcast during the lesson as it allows them to compare podcasts and discuss the features of a good podcast, leading nicely into the main body of learning. With this type of activity you can easily give half of the class (flip a coin) one viewpoint and the other another and they then have to select key points, which leads to the next activity that involves active debate.

'How many ways?'

'How many ways?' are interesting starters and naturally provide differentiated outcomes. For example, issue squared paper to pupils and ask them to decide how many rectangles they can draw with an area of 30cm². This encourages pupils to think. It can be useful for a lesson on area or a lesson on factors. This offers challenge to pupils and you can add a time limit to enhance the competitive element. 'How many ways?' can be used in lots of different subjects. In dance lessons 'show me how many ways you can collapse with your whole body and body parts. Can you collapse quickly? S-l-o-w-l-y? Like a robot'. In PE 'show me how many ways you can stretch your hamstring in a warm-up'. In English a simple example is sentence combining: take two sentences and see how many ways the class can find for combining them into a single sentence (the idea being they explore the use of syntactic possibilities). The key to assessment here is spotting things pupils do the same way and using this as a basis for discussion, selecting any unique examples and then selecting any misconceptions, ensuring that you discuss why these are not correct with pupils. 'How many ways?' can also be used for simple bell-work activities such as, for example, 'how many ways can you make 24 by multiplying two integers together?'

Scenario-based starters

Scenario-based starters develop a story or build up a theme to be developed during the lesson. Pupils engage in an activity where they have to make choices or where they are acting upon an instruction. An example is the jelly baby game often used when teaching population studies. Pupils are given a pot of jelly babies and a set of scenario cards. Each jelly baby colour represents a different cohort within the population structure so that, for example, blue are adult males, orange are adult females, etc. and the scenario cards (for their hypothetical country) are statement-based instructions such as 'lose 50 per cent of the female population through AIDS-related illnesses' (lose 50 per cent of your female population); 'there is an influx of migrant workers' (gain five adult males). The idea being that you move the respective number of jelly babies in and out of the jar depending upon the scenario. As a standalone activity this is task-based and has little learning value. The power is in the discussion – why would one factor cause a given cohort to be reduced or to gain in number? What factors caused population loss? What factors caused population gain? Is this representative of factors globally? Do the factors depend on the region? What factors impact on population? These can be written on a post-it note and then discussed collectively as a whole class. The key is to ensure that pupils are aware of the learning purpose of the activity from the outset and that they know what is expected from them. In this way, when they are 'doing' the activity, they are already thinking and discussing. This type of activity can be differentiated by the activity itself and the different scenarios that pupils have, or it might be differentiation by grouping and role within the group. Some pupils may have prompt cards to support learning and others may be given more challenging scenarios that would include 'what do you think would happen if...' or 'what would be the difference if we introduced x?'. This type of activity can be used where one factor causes an effect.

The list of different styles of starter activity really is endless. Here I have listed just a few that are easy to adapt and implement across different subjects. Most importantly, remember to think about the purpose of the starter activity and the learning outcomes that you want pupils to achieve. Once you have established this then you can determine whether it is necessary for you to differentiate the starter activity and how best to do this to ensure that all pupils are appropriately challenged, can access the learning and achieve success.

Review

The review of any activity is an essential part of the learning process. It allows you to assess where learners are in their personal learning journey and this allows you to direct future learning through differentiation to ensure that pupils make optimum progress. Questioning is probably your most powerful tool in the assessment process. It allows you to probe understanding and to determine any possible misconceptions, which can then be addressed. Do not be afraid to deviate from your lesson plan if your assessment determines that pupils do not quite understand a particular aspect. It is important that this is addressed before moving forwards (although, if it only involves a few pupils, then it may be more appropriate to form a small group to address this aspect while other pupils move to the next activity as, in this way, you are not preventing other pupils from progressing). The review allows you to determine future learning and pupils to assess where they are in relation to success criteria and any areas they need to focus on for improvement. This all forms part of differentiated learning supported by assessment for learning, and the two combined are a powerful tool. Giving pupils the opportunity to reflect on the starter activity is important as this directs their future learning pathway so always ensure that you allow personal reflection time (note that this does not have to be an extended activity).

Remember that if you are using different starters with different pupils then you must think carefully about how you are going to assess these different activities in order to inform future learning. It may be that you use a self- or peer-assessment grid and that you circulate as pupils complete these and then, collectively as a class, you address a few key points to ensure that you are confident that pupils understand the underlying concepts (rather than just ticking and crossing and assuming they have understood). Alternatively, you might choose to sit for a minute or so with each group while they are working and assess the work in this manner (through observation, discussion and questioning), and then perhaps highlight any points of interest when you pull the class back together. Whichever approach you use it is essential that you assess learning and allow time for reflection and that the information you receive is of high quality to inform any future learning pathway.

Start of the lesson: summary

The start of the lesson really is the learning hook. If it is not accessible then pupils will disengage, leading to low level disruption and, often, their attitude to the subject will change to one of 'can't do' and it can sometimes be difficult to change mind sets and re-engage these learners. Therefore always ensure that you match the activity to the needs of the learner and that you use assessment to inform planning. This is essential if learning is to be pitched at just the right level to offer challenge and engagement. Pupils need to be involved in their own learning. Differentiating activities to ensure learning is personalised will encourage pupils to actively participate. Differentiation is such a powerful technique and one that often teachers use naturally in their delivery and interactions with pupils but perhaps need more support on in resource development.

There are lots of different styles of starter activity and we have mentioned only a few in this chapter. Keep in mind that what is most important is not the activity itself but what you do with it, how you use it to inform future planning and how it supports pupils in their own learning. If the activity is 'all singing, all dancing' but has little impact on learning or is one that not all learners can access then there is no point in using it. Always try to think of your audience.

The start of the lesson can take many different structures but remember that pace is important. If an activity is drifting you must stop the activity and regroup as a class (drifting often means it wasn't quite at the right level for the pupils). Never keep 'ploughing on'. The following are examples of structures based on a 60-minute lesson and the timings are a useful guide:

Example 1:

- Bell work (two minutes)
- Share learning outcomes (two minutes)
- Big Question (one minute)
- Starter activity (five minutes)
- Review (two minutes)

Total: 12 minutes

Example 2:

- Share learning outcomes (two minutes)
- Big Question (three minutes)
- Starter activity (five minutes)
- Review (two minutes)

Total: 12 minutes

Example 3:

- Big Question (five minutes)
- Learning outcomes (two minutes)

- Starter activity (five minutes)
- Review (two minutes)

Total: 14 minutes

Example 4:

- Learning outcomes (two minutes)
- Big Question (five minutes)

Total: 7 minutes

You must determine what works best for you in your classroom and I would advise mixing it up. The very best teachers really do vary the approach they take. This keeps learners on their toes and makes the lessons interesting. Below are a few key questions I always encourage teachers to think about:

- How do pupils arrive to your lesson (staggered arrival, line up outside)?
- Are you greeting pupils as they arrive?
- Have you planned a simple bell work activity and is this something pupils can just 'get on with'?
- Is this bell work personalised or a generic task?
- Do you have clear learning outcomes stating the aspect of learning and the context?
- Do pupils know and understand the success criteria or progress markers?
- Do you have these pre-prepared for pupils to stick into their books or are they kept visible at all times and returned to at key assessment opportunities?
- Have you planned a Big Question that will allow you to assess the progress of all learners?
- Is this differentiated? If so, how?
- Have you prepared a starter activity that links to the learning and that will lead to the next learning cycle?
- Can all pupils access the starter activity?
- Is the starter activity differentiated (it does not have to be) and, if so, how have you allocated pupils to different activities?
- Have you planned an appropriate assessment strategy and will this allow you and pupils to know their starting point?
- Does this data inform differentiation in the main body of the lesson? How?
- Have you thought of targeted questioning and are you prepared to 'bounce' these around the classroom?
- Do you have an awareness of any misconceptions that may arise?
- Can you move forwards in the lesson plan or do you need to change direction?

Differentiation for learning in the main body of the lesson

Assessment of the starter activity should provide sufficient information to inform the main body of the lesson and should be used as a platform to launch learning. Pupils need to be aware of the progress they have made towards achieving learning outcomes or success criteria, and of any areas of strength and/or weakness, and this should be used to develop learning in the lesson. Each pupil is different. They have different learning needs, different interests and different levels of readiness to learn. This could lead to a complicated mix with a class of 30 pupils, which is why it is important to employ strategies to support you and the pupils in the classroom. Differentiation should enhance learning and the learning experience and support pupils in maximising progress. We must involve pupils in mapping their own learning pathway as this involvement allows them to achieve a much greater depth of understanding.

The main body of the lesson can consist of a single learning cycle (with an extended activity) or a sequence of shorter learning cycles. The structure of the lesson very much depends on the topic, the resources you are using and, of course, your audience (the pupils). What is most important is that you match activities to the needs of the pupils to ensure that every pupil can access learning and make progress during the lesson. This is key to differentiation and this is something teachers often overlook. It is not necessarily that you have lots of different activities going on (perhaps to satisfy an observer), but that those activities are pitched at the right level and, indeed, delivered through the correct medium to ensure all pupils can make progress. Remember that it is not necessary for activities or lessons to be 'all-singing, all-dancing' in order for learning to be outstanding. What is key to success is involving pupils in the learning process; something outstanding teachers do as part of their daily practice.

During the main body of the lesson pupils develop key concepts, key processes and thinking skills: information-processing skills, reasoning skills, enquiry skills, creative-thinking skills and evaluation skills (though perhaps not all in the same lesson). In using activities that promote thinking skills pupils learn to learn, they know 'how' as well as 'what' and, in the moments of reflection, they think about thinking (meta-cognition). Assessment and differentiation therefore go hand in hand and supplement each other to create an optimum learning environment. Assessment is essential as we and learners need to know starting points, levels of comprehension and where pupils are in relation to learning outcomes (mapping individual progress); this information may be used to direct future learning (either during the lesson or at a point later in time). Without assessing each activity all we do is move from activity to activity without knowing whether the learning intentions or the success criteria associated with each activity have been met, and we have little concept of whether we are travelling along the correct path. Indeed without assessing learning we cannot direct next steps and therefore cannot differentiate or match learning needs. We have no awareness of 'where learners are' and cannot create a learning profile. This effectively means pupils just 'do' and it reduces the likelihood of pupils developing the same depth of understanding or involvement in their own learning as they do when we use formative assessment (active assessment during the learning process not after it) alongside differentiation practices. In other words, our lessons become task-driven. Unless assessment is an integral part of the learning process pupils will not think about learning (and consequently we cannot demonstrate outstanding practice) and it is the outcomes of these mini-assessments that inform and support differentiation – guiding pupils to appropriate learning pathways. The information we source can be used to encourage pupils to make choices in their learning. It also provides us with insight into the level of support that pupils need from us or other resources to make progress. No one size fits all and if we move to an environment where we truly personalise learning we must be conscious that we do so in a managed way to avoid a chaotic and frenzied classroom where little learning actually takes place. A fine balance is needed. It would be unrealistic for a teacher teaching five classes per day (that's potentially 150 pupils through their door on a daily basis) to fully personalise learning – with each pupil following an individualised plan. This is why skilful differentiation techniques must be employed to ensure that we can optimise learning and provide suitable pathways for learners in a manageable environment. This means carefully planned resources that support learning, with further differentiation through our interactions and discussions with individual pupils as we circulate (something we do naturally without thinking).

When we sequence activities they need to build on previous work or develop learning in different ways. Some pupils may follow a single cycle whereas other pupils may require more support and follow a parallel structure of two or more learning cycles. Assessment underpins this choice and does not have to be an explicit activity; equally important is the minute-by-minute ongoing assessment that we make as professionals and that a pupil makes of their own learning. Assessment drives differentiated pathways in learning and we must always be aware of the close and important relationship between the two. In this chapter we focus on different types of activities that are often used in the main body of the lesson and discuss opportunities for differentiation (sharing ideas across a range of subjects). The aim is not to be prescriptive but to provide you with a source of ideas that you can adapt and use to best effect in your lessons that are tailored to the pupils in your classroom. Remember the point I keep emphasising: one outstanding teacher can teach in a very different way to another – your job is to find your own style and one that you can adapt to your audience.

Sequencing the learning

We all know that things don't always go to plan and that sometimes our most meticulously planned lessons just don't go as we expected. We know that we must always be flexible but, in reality, some teachers stick rigidly to a plan in order to cover content driven by the curriculum. Sometimes pupils surprise us with how they adapt to a particular topic and sometimes our brightest pupils 'just don't get it'; yet we must be able to adapt to every eventuality, redirecting learning where appropriate. Differentiation is an essential part of the learning process, supporting learners in accessing the curriculum. Often teachers differentiate solely based upon prior data (for example, they have already pre-assigned pupils to different worksheets before the lesson has even begun) so I must add a note of caution – data supports learning but, make no mistake, we are dealing with human beings who by their nature are not quite so predictable; lots of different factors out of our control affect their attitude to learning on a daily basis. Use any data you have as a tool to support planning but don't make the common mistake of using it to pre-assign pupils to a specific pathway (pre-determining learning). This is not good practice. Data is a guide. You must use mini-assessments during the lesson, your observation and pupils' self-assessment to determine learning pathways and next steps. I use the example from mathematics: a pupil can excel in algebra and number but have limited spatial awareness. Therefore if they were pre-assigned to a 'high' level pathway owing to their performance in number (assessed in the last summative assessment) then this would perhaps not work when applied to a topic within shape, space and measure where the pupil may require a more supportive framework. Note, further, that two pupils of similar ability (and motivation to learn) given the same information may cope differently depending on their background knowledge. No one pupil is less able than the other but the same learner will make more of an explanation of a familiar topic than of a less-familiar topic. Mini-assessments during the lesson would highlight the most appropriate pathway, which is why their use in lessons to guide differentiation is essential.

During the main body of the lesson we develop concepts. This phase is typically over 50 per cent of the lesson, so it is important to think how you are going to structure learning: are some pupils going to follow a single learning cycle that develops understanding through a more independent approach? Are some pupils going to follow a parallel but more structured pathway consisting two or more learning cycles that scaffolds learning? Be conscious of the fact that this is often the phase in the lesson where teachers revert to the 'I do, you do, we do' lecture style of teaching, where teachers tell pupils how to do something (typically through demonstration), pupils then follow the recipe and complete a series of questions. This requires little thinking and limits development and is where planning becomes important. Not to prescribe a rigid plan but to think about how we introduce and develop key concepts in learning. A starting point is to think about the end point and then work backwards to 'chunk' the learning. What do we want pupils to learn or understand by the end of the lesson? How can we develop this to different depths for different groups or types of learners? How might we develop this through a single or more structured pathway? What are the key learning flags or progression markers? By focusing on what we want pupils to learn we can develop activities to support this process. At key points in the lesson (perhaps following each activity – although progress checks can occur during an activity) mini-assessments act as a tool to check understanding and readiness to 'move on'. They support differentiation and they need to be carefully designed to check that the key concept has been understood and to detect any misconceptions. Pupils need to be involved in the assessment process and it is important that we allow for reflection (remember all parts of the learning cycle, no matter what stage we are at, must be completed to support learning). Simply knowing a numerical score (when pupils are 'tested') does not tell us very much and we need to think carefully about the questions that we ask to probe understanding (we address assessment in Chapter 6 and questioning in Chapter 7).

As teachers we very much facilitate learning by providing opportunities for pupils to develop their thinking. When you plan lessons you must therefore plan for learning rather than plan what you are going to teach. There is a very subtle difference. If our focus is on learning, then we are thinking about the pupils in our classroom; if we are focusing on what we are going to teach then we are thinking about our own delivery and can easily revert to a directive approach. Indeed the definition of the word 'teach' is to 'impart knowledge to or instruct (someone) as to how to do something' (www.oxforddictionaries.com) or 'to cause (someone) to learn something by example or experience'. The focus seems to be on the direct relation between teacher and pupils. It is of course the weighting on learning that develops a pupil's understanding and love of a subject and this should form the focus of our planning.

So, the underlying question is: how do we develop activities in this phase of the lesson that encourage pupils to think for themselves? One of the techniques I use is to remind myself that if I am about to tell a pupil something then I think consciously about how I can turn this into a question that will encourage the pupil to think for themselves and arrive at a solution (this may not be the correct solution but it will encourage learning debate). In developing this technique you require no additional resources; it is simply about you and your ability to create a learning dialogue in your classroom through clever questioning or your ability to use resources in a slightly different way adjusted to the needs of the pupils.

For every learning outcome or success criteria it is important to think about how you will encourage pupils to develop their thinking skills and how you will develop an activity to embed key concepts and assess progression. We therefore need to focus on how we introduce concepts, which typically occurs in the main body of the lesson rather than the starter (usually used for benchmarking) or plenary. Following the introduction of concepts it is important to use a mini-assessment to determine progress – this is then embedded in the main assessment activity. In the remainder of this section we discuss how we can introduce key concepts (the examples are kept simple and this is because I want to demonstrate the technique rather than subject content) and where we may need to take a differentiated approach. I encourage you to think carefully about the very powerful quote by Benjamin Franklin when you plan for learning: 'Tell me and I forget, teach me and I may remember, involve me and I learn'.

Let us consider an example from English: introducing similes. Rather than telling pupils the definition of a simile, providing a few examples and then getting pupils to complete an exercise, encourage pupils to think for themselves. You can differentiate this activity by giving some pupils similes in 'less-complicated' sentences, for example:

- Her hair was as soft as a spider web.
- The river flows like a stream of glass.
- The town square was buzzing like a beehive.

For those who are more-able readers provide similes in more complicated sentences, for example:

- He had hidden his wealth, heaped and hoarded and piled on high like sacks of wheat in a granary.
- Barefooted, ragged, with neglected hair, she was a thin slip of a girl, like a new moon.
- She was like a modest flower blown in sunny June and warm as sun at noon's high hour.

Ask pupils what they notice about the sentences they have been given; the purpose being to raise discussion about comparing one thing to another using 'as', 'as a…' or 'like…' but, at this point, don't give them the definition of 'simile'. What commonalities do they spot? What are the key language features? You can ask pupils to engage in paired discussion or small-group discussion at this point. Then ask pupils to write a single sentence describing an image (provide a variety of different images) based on the sentence structure they have discussed as pairs or groups (this encourages them to debate together and compare). What features of their sentence make them similar to the three sentences they were given? How do they know? Swap with another pair or group and exchange constructive comments. Place the images up on the board one by one and ask each pair or group to state their sentence and the reason behind it. Once everyone has commented on their image then ask the class to discuss what they think they have developed. Can they now define a simile? This leads to discussion and your input comes only to direct questioning and to ensure that pupils are aware of the correct definition and vocabulary (i.e. the use of the word 'simile'). This can be followed by a simple mini-assessment with three sentences where pupils need to identify the simile.

This type of technique can be used in any subject and the basis is to ensure pupils think. When we tell people things they tend to forget but when we involve them in the process they are much more likely to retain any information. In mathematics, for example, rather than telling pupils a rule encourage them to determine it. To experience the process I ask you to complete the following example. Given:

- $-5 \times -3 = 15$
- $7 \times 5 = 35$
- $-6 \times 4 = -24$
- $8 \times -4 = -32$
- $-7 \times -7 = 49$
- $9 \times -2 = -18$

What's the rule?

Immediately you are thinking. You are looking at the numbers and trying to make a connection. You are involved in the process. Hopefully you have come up with the general rule. Now answer the following quick-fire questions (this is best done on mini-whiteboards so that you can see everyone's answer and you can then target questioning accordingly):

1) -7×8
2) -3×-3
3) 9×-10

If, however, I had listed 'rules' on the board: $+ \times + = +; - \times - = +; + \times - = -; - \times + = -$, and then asked you the same questions – most likely you would refer back to the board and, if we are honest, most pupils start to switch off (some don't even listen) because they are being asked to memorise and recall a rule or are being 'talked at'. Involvement in learning is key to engaging learners. Of course, as presented above, the activity is not differentiated; to differentiate an activity such as this you may give some pupils more challenging multiplications in the three quick-fire questions, such as -15×13 or $-3 \times 5 \times -7$. The key is not necessarily knowing multiplication tables (although we obviously want pupils to know them) but being able to understand how to multiply positive and negative numbers so, if some pupils require support (perhaps the less able) with the actual times-tables, then provide them with a multiplication grid (while this may go against the grain for many mathematicians, remember we can test recall of times-tables at another point – the purpose of this activity is to understand how to multiply positive and negative numbers).

Take a simple example from physics – circuits. Often teachers demonstrate circuits. However, instead of telling pupils how to ensure electricity flows through a complete circuit and 'teaching' them the concept, allow pupils to explore. Place several different circuits around the room and ask pupils to go to specific circuits (number them and pupils will visit four different set-ups in pairs) and explore how, for example, to make a light bulb light. You can easily differentiate this by having more complicated circuits and directing the more able to more challenging circuits. The power in this activity then comes through the discussion, your use of questioning and the questions that arise from the pupils themselves. Before you summarise and for-malise language (terminology) or technical aspects you can then ask different groups of pupils to work on a different problem – this encourages thinking. When you are confident that pupils have gained from the experience you can bring the whole class back together to share ideas and to summarise the activity.

Introducing concepts in this way removes the initial direct teacher input and develops deeper learning. It can be adapted for any topic and any subject and is easily differentiated – all that's required is a little thought. You can most likely adapt existing resources rather than create new ones. If you were going to tell pupils something then simply think about how you can encourage them to think for themselves first. Also, remember that this type of activity will not necessarily generate perfect answers – it's not meant to. Misconceptions are equally powerful and we often develop great learn-ing through unpicking them. What it does do is encourage pupils to think; it involves them in the learning process.

Mini-assessments

Mini-assessments act as a progress checker during the lesson and should be used to check understanding at key points. They form part of the information that determines next steps for pupils (possibly differentiated pathways) and so they play an essential part in the learning process. Teachers typically use them to determine whether suc-cess criteria have been met but it needs to go beyond a tick-box exercise. Think about why you are assessing – what it will tell you, what it will tell pupils and what outcomes does it work towards? As a result of the mini-assessment are you aware of where pupils are in their learning (perhaps their progress on a learning ladder)? Are pupils aware of where they are? Does this provide sufficient information to direct next steps in learning? Very often teachers 'bolt-on' a mini-assessment (for the sake of it) – gaining very little from the process. The quality of the assessment is essential. Asking pupils five questions, marking them and then relaying a numerical score will provide you with little information (other than a mark out of five). It doesn't tell you the depth of understanding – this will only be gained from probing questions. So how you mark the questions is very important; probing questions will allow you to determine whether pupils have grasped the underlying concepts and these can be targeted and differentiated. The same applies to peer assessment. Often teachers stop activities and allow pupils to mark a partner's work under the guise of peer assess-ment without thinking about the quality of that assessment. Pupils simply swapping and marking work has limited, if any, learning value. Therefore, equally important to planning an engaging activity is to plan how you are going to assess that activity, deciding what information that assessment provides and how it will inform you and pupils of their next step to maximise progress in learning (differentiated pathways).

When you use a brief questioning session as a mini-assessment then best practice is to bounce questions from one pupil to the next rather than from pupil to you and back (use basketball rather than ping-pong questioning – that is, pass the question around the class to develop the answer – perhaps injecting thought provokers). These can then be easily differentiated and you can target questioning to individual pupils as necessary. For example, during the learning phase you may have had a discussion with a pupil struggling with a particular aspect and wish to direct a quick-fire question to them to determine whether they have now resolved the misconception or problem and then bounce this around the classroom (we discuss questioning techniques in Chapter 7 but I emphasise here that you must ask the whole class the question, allow thinking time and then select the pupil to respond – otherwise pupils will switch off if they know they don't have to answer). You may want to challenge learning further in a whole-class environment and ask questions to move thinking forwards or in a different direction. Alternatively, if you ask all pupils a series of, for example, five quick-fire questions to be answered on mini-whiteboards (allowing whole class simultaneous assessment) remember it is not 'seeing' the correct answer that tells you whether pupils have a good understanding, but through your use of questioning following the answers. If, for example, pupils give different answers that equate to the same thing it is good to discuss which is better and why, or why it doesn't matter. An example from mathematics that demonstrates this is if I asked pupils a quick-fire question such as, 'simplify: $5a + 7b - 3b - 4a$' and the following responses are received '$a + 4b$', '$4b + a$' and '$1a + 4b$'. Discussions would explore whether all of these expressions mean the same thing. Should we write a or $1a$? Does it matter how we order the terms? So this simple single question could give rise to more branched questions. Indeed, subsequent verbal questioning to assess understanding should lead to at least three springboard questions from every direct question, thus ensuring that at least 20 pupils have made a contribution.

Pair-matching exercises are commonly used as a mini-assessment activity and these are an excellent way to differentiate the assessment activity. You can give all pupils a similar activity but to differing degrees of complexity or support. It is therefore important to create your own or to tailor any prepared resources to the needs of your learners. Alternatively, not all pupils have to do the same activity and you may choose to use different pair-matching activities to target different concepts or areas of development. This is useful if you use the activities in a different way, perhaps to accommodate different learning styles offering much greater opportunities for personalised learning. You may leave, for example, one box blank and ask pupils to fill it in. Several examples of pair-matching and matching exercises were illustrated in Chapter 3.

Other examples of mini-assessments that work well are comparative activities. These compare two or more pieces of work; one of which is 'good' and one of which is 'poor' and one in between the two. Pupils can work individually, in pairs or in small groups to highlight key areas. The most important part of this type of activity is in the explanations: the 'whys'. Why is one piece better than another? What does the other piece need to do to improve? This enables you to determine the quality of pupils' understanding and, if you tailor it to the success criteria of your previous activity, then you can determine whether they have been met and the quality of understanding. Keep in mind that in some subjects, typically the more creative, the good example might only be one of many and that there are lots of alternatives. This activity is then ideal for differentiation as you can target different pupils or groups of pupils with different pieces to compare (usually differentiating by task (ability)). Reviewing work during the learning has much greater impact than looking at 'good' work at the end of the lesson. Why? Because pupils can act upon it to improve their own work (at the end of the lesson, as a 'here's what you should have done', common sense tells us that this is too late to have any impact on learning). This type of activity provides a lot of information when assessing pupil progress and can be used to determine readiness to move on to the next steps in learning.

To summarise:

- use mini-assessments to support learning and to determine learning pathways;
- involve pupils in the assessment process and in choosing their next steps;
- differentiate, for example, through task, resource and questioning;
- re-direct learning if the mini-assessment highlights any misconceptions;
- only move on when the concept is secure.

The main assessment activity

Once we have introduced the key concepts, and assessed pupil learning through mini-assessments, lessons typically progress to a main activity. This usually combines concepts or skills acquired during the lesson and determines pupils' ability to apply their learning (traditionally referred to as the main activity). All of the information we and pupils acquire from the mini-assessments allows pupils to choose (with your support) the appropriate main activity. This serves to embed learning and encourages pupils to reflect. There are lots of different activities that embed learning and these should typically be longer in duration than the activities so far, allowing pupils space for thinking time and time to process their learning. You will know when the time is right to draw the activity to a close for feedback and review, judging this by observation or learning dialogue during the learning phase. Quality not quantity is important here. In the next section we look at different types of activities, when and if it is appropriate to differentiate and how we can do this to best effect.

The worksheet

You will often see teachers differentiate by task – allocating pupils to one of three different worksheets (usually colour-coded green, amber or red). Sometimes these are superficially assigned, or pupils get used to always being given a particular colour and so pick that one anyway with little thought or, worse, they choose red because they think it will be the easy option for them. None of this is overly good practice. If you are differentiating in this way then three worksheets is reasonable – particularly in terms of teacher workload. How you tailor and style these worksheets, however, needs careful thought and, because you are preparing them in advance of the lesson, it is important to think about the types of learners in the particular class and their learning needs or preferences. Colour-coding worksheets (while convenient perhaps for the teacher) can be disheartening for pupils who are, for example, always red. I advise that you mix it up and use shapes, letters or words (for example, names of space shuttles, names of animals, etc.) for different worksheets and that the outcomes of the mini-assessments, combined with pupil choice and your support, determine the particular worksheet for an individual based on performance at that point in time and during that particular lesson. Remember that pre-assigning pupils to different pathways based on prior assessment data alone can limit progress and means that we apply a 'glass ceiling', which never allows some pupils to develop. Labelling pupils in this way can not only limit their progress but impact on their motivation. Choice should be made based on performance at that particular time, combined with the outcomes of the mini-assessments, your professional judgement and the pupil's assessment of their own learning. This is how we begin to challenge learning although, obviously, if you know that a pupil has made an unsuitable choice then you may want to guide their selection and offer a little advice.

In designing worksheets best practice is to ensure that the worksheets all lead to the same learning outcome but do so in a differentiated way – some requiring greater depth or application of knowledge. It's not about giving the less able 'simpler work' but about making the work accessible to those who may need more support in their learning. For instance, some pupils may require more support with applied questions and it may be necessary to scaffold the question (splitting it into several parts) on one worksheet and, on another, to pose the question in a direct way (without any scaffolding or hints). This gives the more-able pupils more challenge and, at the same time, allows weaker pupils to access the same question. Similarly, on one sheet you may have a series of hints or have a sheet of hints prepared so that if pupils need additional support they can ask for the hint sheet. There is no problem with doing this as long as the hint sheet still encourages pupils to think. Essentially what we are doing is thinking about the conceptual and information-processing demands of each task and designing materials where we gradually increase the onus on the pupil. In PE a question such as 'what are the key principles when planning a training programme?' might be too challenging for all pupils and some may need a framework to support learning, thus:

The key principles of planning a training programme are:
Specificity – ...
Overload – ...
Progression – ...
Reversibility – ...
We use FITT to add details:
Frequency – ...
Intensity – ...
Time – ...
Type – ...

1. Find the area of the shaded region.

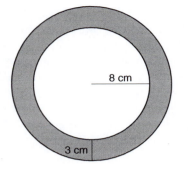

Figure 4.1 Find the area of the shaded region.

Figures 4.1 and 4.2 show an example from mathematics with the question in Figure 4.2 scaffolded to support learning. Pupils requiring a more structured approach to support learning would be given this question, with the aim being that any worksheet would progress to less structure (less guided input).

A second example is shown in Figure 4.3 and Figure 4.4, where pupils are guided through the question in Figure 4.4 in a way they are not in Figure 4.3.

Some teachers still prefer to use a single worksheet. Whether you do this or use several worksheets, encourage pupils to choose the questions that they answer and avoid working sequentially through questions. If pupils can do one or two correctly of a particular type of question and are confident then they should be expected to move to the next type of question that offers them more challenge. Remember that it is not necessary to do 20 similar questions if pupils are able to confidently and correctly complete two or three and can explain clearly what they have done (some

1) Calculate the area of a circle with radius 8 cm.
2) Calculate the area of a circle with radius 11 cm.
3) How would you use this information to calculate the
   area of the shaded region in the diagram below?
4) Now find the area of the shaded region.

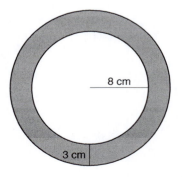

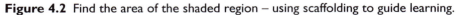

Figure 4.2 Find the area of the shaded region – using scaffolding to guide learning.

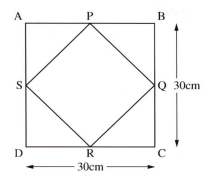

The square PQRS is made by joining the midpoints of the square ABCD.

The square ABCD has sides of length 30cm.

Calculate the length of one side of the square PQRS.

Figure 4.3 An applied question with no scaffolding.

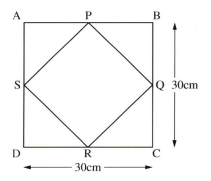

1) What is the midpoint of a line?

2) What is the length of CQ and QB?

3) Explain your answer.

4) Sketch the triangle RCQ and label the length of the sides that you know.

5) Calculate the length of RQ.

Figure 4.4 An applied question with structured support.

teachers measure volume of work completed with understanding and the two are not synonymous). Also remember that we do not need 'more of the same' – if we have made a good assessment during a mini-assessment then this does not need to be repeated in the same way on the worksheet. The purpose of a lesson is to progress in learning and we must keep this in mind when sequencing learning and activities.

Video/podcast

Using digital devices, whether as a creative tool (where pupils create their own video or podcast) or as a source for learning (where they use a video or podcast as part of the learning or information-gathering process), is something that pupils seem to readily engage with. These types of activities, however, require careful planning and management skills. Dependent on your school usage policy or bring-your-own-device policy, mobile phones, video cameras and iPads can all be used to create videos and, if you liaise with your school IT department, they will no doubt be able to advise you on the various packages to which they already subscribe (there are also many free apps that can be used). Whichever you use I would recommend familiarising yourself with the software beforehand. In addition, it is important that pupils are trained in what you are expecting them to do. Do they know what constitutes a good video or podcast? What are the key features? Can they use the software? One thing I often recommend doing when you first introduce video production in the classroom is a simple starter activity that focuses on quality. Prepare two videos (or three), keep them brief (two minutes each) and ask pupils to compare them. The idea being that, collectively, you develop a series of 'do's and don'ts' or a good and bad checklist. Pupils can then use this when developing their own videos. Include things like camera angle, speed of talking, quality of the script, language, and so on.

There are many uses of videos in learning. Below we discuss possible ways of using video technology in your classroom combined with differentiation strategies:

1) Creating videos or podcasts: when pupils create videos or podcasts they usually work in small groups. This is an ideal opportunity to differentiate by role. For example: script, designer, reporter, cameraman and so on. If there are particular skills pupils need to develop then they can be allocated to a specific role. When pupils create videos it is extremely important that each role is assessed and that there is the opportunity to watch or use the video. The final production is a contribution of all roles and pupils must work together to create the product. An important part when reflecting on this type of activity is the positive contribution of each pupil. It is important that each pupil is given some positive feedback from other members of the group, and that they have the opportunity to reflect on this and to think about how they might have developed the role. The videos themselves need to be watched and they can, for example, all be based upon different research areas, so that the rest of the class then have to answer a question based upon the video they watch, or they can be for revision purposes or

designed for those new to the topic, for example, year 8 producing a video for year 5 pupils on ratio. We are naturally assessing both the skill and the content. We know that pupils learn when they teach – this is mainly because they have to process information and relay it to a third party in such a way as to develop understanding (they are thinking about thinking – increased cognitive ability) – and so producing a video is a different way of getting pupils to think and to articulate and present their thinking (explanation is a higher order thinking skill).

2) Watching a video or listening to a podcast is another way of using media in the classroom. Think carefully about how you are going to do this. I recommend allowing pupils to watch the video through once initially (making no comments and keeping it short – five minutes maximum). Then issue pupils with a question – try to make it something that encourages them to think and that is not directly answered in the video, but something that leads to them forming argument and identifying any additional information they may need (otherwise, if you ask them a direct question that is answered in the video they switch off once they have got the answer to their particular question). In terms of differentiating it is best to give certain pupils different questions. Don't identify who has the same question at this point. Allow pupils to re-watch the video and then to jot down their thoughts individually. Then encourage them to find a person with the same question (perhaps put a shape in the corner of the piece of paper and those with the same shape form a new pair). Allow a brief period (two minutes) for discussion and then ask all pupils with the same shape to go to a specific table where they form a new group. This group then work as a team, discussing their individual thoughts and the thoughts from their paired discussions to formulate a response to the question. Videos without sound are often very powerful in this type of activity and you can ask pupils to write a 'script' for the silent film. When pupils watch without sound and they only have one sense to focus on they tend to watch the film more closely (often with sound and visual they will be distracted and rely on the sound for information and gaze elsewhere). Silent film can be used, for example, in mathematics. Video yourself finding the bearing of one point from another (do each step very carefully) and then ask pupils to think carefully about what you did, offering their argument for 'why'. This type of activity offers natural differentiation. However, you can of course ask different groups of pupils to watch different videos (when the video is silent this is very easily done using laptops or tablet devices). Pupils can then use their findings to produce their own video answering a specific challenging question. The video is not necessarily a presentation of their final answer but can be an assimilation of clips demonstrating a work in progress, which may include how they overcame particular misconceptions and so on.

Computer activities

Computer activities provide an ideal environment for personalised learning. It is, of course, how you use computers to develop learning that is important and then how you assess that learning to ensure that each pupil is following a pathway that they can access (differentiation) but that, at the same time, challenges their thinking. When we design a lesson that involves pupils working independently on computers we do so to enhance the learning experience, yet often when we observe the use of ICT in lessons it does very little to develop learning (worse it acts negatively by evoking low-level behavioural issues). This can be because of low teacher confidence, poor planning, pupils not placing any value on the activity (thinking it is not a proper lesson), the activity being boring or not appropriately timed and a lack of focus.

The key to using computers in lessons is to ensure that there is a specific learning outcome, which is decontextualised from the skill, and that pupils are very aware of the learning purpose and of how the computer supports them in achieving it. In other words, they need to be very clear of the assessment criteria for the activity, allowing them to assess their own progress at key points and to be aware that you are assessing their learning (perhaps through an additional overarching question that they need to answer towards the end of the activity – a mini-Big Question). Pace is a key aspect. If you allow the activity to drag then pupils will start to disengage and, of course, this will lead to them playing with the computer mouse or perhaps surfing the internet, rocking on chairs or messaging each other and so on. This is why careful planning, clear expectations (and rules), timing and challenge are essential (along with a sensible seating plan). It is therefore very important, both for a mixed-ability class and a 'set' class, that the activity is differentiated and matched to the needs of each learner, offering the appropriate degree of challenge (not just an extension task with more of the same) that engages each individual pupil in the classroom.

This can be done by giving pupils different activities or different resources. For example, if the aim is to research a particular topic then you might give some pupils a list of resources that are quite challenging to interpret (perhaps more advanced internet sources) and other pupils websites that provide the information in a simpler format (thus allowing all pupils to access the material). Taking this one step further, there might be sources that are more suitable for a visual learner (perhaps illustrations or diagrams) or some that are more interactive (suiting the kinaesthetic learner). Thinking about what you want pupils to achieve and knowing their respective starting points (skills and knowledge-based) allows you to work backwards – planning for learning by thinking about how involving the computer in the process will optimise the experience.

Other uses of computer resources may simply be programmes that your subject subscribes to such as MyMaths (www.mymaths.co.uk) where topics are levelled and pupils can complete activities at a level that is appropriate to them – the computer 'marks' their work (a numerical score). While such programmes offer a personalised approach (in its global meaning), there is still the danger that, in using these programmes, pupils read an example and then complete a series of questions while never really actively engaging in the thinking process and not being challenged as to the 'why'. Therefore, always give pupils an additional question that relies on them being able to interpret and apply their newly acquired knowledge. Of course this is an opportunity for further differentiation and you may scaffold the question for some learners or give different learners, individually or in pairs or small groups, different challenge questions. However you do this the important point is that you then assess the learning so that the activity is valued and that pupils know that simply going through the motions and completing an activity is not the purpose. The purpose is for them to acquire new knowledge or skills and to be able to apply these to a challenging question, to discuss their learning in the wider context and to assess their progress (both self- and peer-assessment), thinking carefully about any gaps in their learning and their next steps. This ensures that differentiation supports learning.

Computers also provide support in subjects by saving time – allowing the focus to be on a specific aspect. For example if, in a science lesson, pupils are completing a series of experiments and they have to plot the results on different graphs, then the main purpose is to interpret the graph and think about the scientific explanation, and plotting the graph on paper may take considerable time (for some pupils this may dominate the lesson). Computers can speed up this process and allow the focus to be on the primary goal. This means that valuable learning time is not lost. Pupils simply input their data and the graph is generated. They can focus on interpretation and explaining their results. The skill of plotting a graph can be developed in another lesson (or in mathematics in a cross–curricular link), or may already be a skill that is acquired but the key learning outcomes are addressed in sufficient time by using the computer (and not rushed or side-lined by the considerable time graphing on paper can take pupils).

Computers or tablet devices are excellent for all types of learner. They enable pupils to experience learning in a way that was previously not possible. For example, seeing pictures of the international space station does not compare with using the 3D tour available on the NASA website (www.nasa.gov) where pupils can explore the space station freely. This is far more engaging and promotes questions and excellent discussion. The same is true for atomic structure in chemistry or parts of the body in biology, where 3D imaging allows us to explore. Where we use visual or audio materials of this nature we can differentiate in the physical materials that pupils use (differentiation by resource) or through the questions we expect them to be able to answer as part of the learning process (differentiation by task). This may involve pupils working individually, in pairs or collectively in groups. The possibilities are endless but what is important is that the learning remains focused and purposeful with pupils clear on what they are trying to achieve. In languages, you may use video in such a way as a 'what comes next' activity. Pupils can watch a short clip and they then have to design the next stage – this may be a narrative or a piece of drama. This makes learning more interesting and, while it does not change the material being 'taught', it changes the way in which pupils experience the learning, their interaction and their engagement.

The focus on computers to engage boys (particularly those who show low levels of interest in reading and writing) has been highlighted by a recent report (www.bbc.co.uk/news/education-27936946).

The use of Minecraft (https://minecraft.net) in lessons to develop creative writing – pupils use the game to create new scenes or scenarios and this helps them to visualise – has proved positive. While there is debate over the use of computer games in the classroom it is worth remembering that many of us use game-based activities (non-computer based) and that really the only difference is technology and the classroom management skills that run alongside. The key to successful use of any technology (and software) in your classroom is that you are familiar with it – you know the potential pitfalls and how to overcome them. It is also important to manage the activity effectively, thus:

• Are pupils aware of the learning outcome (skill- and context-defined)?
• Do they know the success criteria?
• Do they know what is expected of them?
• Is the task timed (to remove drift)?
• Is the task focused?
• Is the task relevant?
• Do pupils have the necessary skills to use the technology?
• Are pupils working individually or in pairs?
• Does the use of technology actually enhance learning?

Textbooks

It is difficult to differentiate using a textbook as, by their nature, they are a generic resource. I personally don't use textbooks as, while they 'list' key curriculum needs, they are not tailored to the learners in my classroom (they are a global resource). They are, however, a good source of ideas when you are creating different worksheets or as a source of images or diagrams for pupils to view (these are professional and often very clear for pupils), based upon which you can ask specific targeted questions. If you do use textbooks regularly then you must really think about how you are using them. If it is simply a case of pupils completing the questions then this is not best practice. One suggestion is to allow pupils to choose the questions they answer or, alternatively, you design three different pathways based upon the outcomes to the mini-assessments. What is important is that all pupils access the applied questions that typically occur at the end of the exercise. This then doesn't disadvantage or limit the progress of those who are perhaps slower at working than others (but no less able). If you allow differentiation by outcome to be determined by pace, those who are no less able than another but who work at a slower pace will not be sufficiently challenged (as they may not reach the higher-order questions that typically occur at the end of an exercise).

Investigations and rich tasks

An investigation is essentially a complex task that is based on challenging and authentic questions or problems, and that involves pupils in design, problem-solving, decision-making, or research activities. It gives pupils the opportunity to work relatively autonomously over extended periods of time culminating in realistic products or presentations. In reality, however, we guide investigations and research-based or rich tasks and this is mainly owing to time factors; we are, in many respects, constrained by a curriculum and an exam- or content-driven culture. In other words, we don't allow true investigations but encourage pupils to investigate different aspects over a period (usually extended beyond a single lesson) typically steered to a particular outcome. What we are really doing is developing investigative skills for independent research later in pupil's academic or work-based careers. Investigations are an essential part of our curriculum if we are to develop enquiring minds and learners who are independent, and who are able to think and synthesise information from different sources leading to a carefully considered and evidenced conclusion.

So what does an investigative task actually do? I believe it:

- allows pupils to explore the subject using a variety of different methods in intriguing contexts;
- encourages pupils to pose as well as solve problems, make conjectures and ask questions of themselves and each other;
- allows pupils to extend knowledge or apply knowledge in new contexts at a range of levels;
- broadens their thinking skills and deepens their content knowledge;
- reveals underlying principles or connections between different areas within the subject and potentially across a range of subjects.

Investigations are equally applicable to all subjects from the arts to the sciences and should be integrated into the curriculum as appropriate (remember though that some areas within a specific subject will be more open to a research-based investigation). What is common is that they need to be carefully planned. So, when should we use investigations to support learning? Some teachers use investigations to promote intrigue at the start of a series of lessons and to generate a series of ideas or questions that need to be answered as study progresses. This allows pupils (individually and collectively) to form assessment criteria against which they can measure progress (tangible and pupil-generated evidence) and tailor their own research. Others use investigations at the end of a topic to determine whether pupils have understood key concepts and are able to apply their learning in a different and wider context (perhaps involving a combination of previous and newly acquired skills or subject knowledge) and some possibly combine this with more research-based home learning activities. These are all of equal value and should be used as part of the learning process to create situations where we challenge pupils and encourage them to develop their thinking skills independently.

Many argue that differentiation occurs through outcome and this is of course true. The different outcomes generated by pupils or groups of pupils will develop at different rates and depths and this occurs if all pupils are given exactly the same statement to research and the same level of support. However, owing to the fact that most of our investigations in school are, in reality, structured, there is an argument for the differentiation of this type of activity and it can encompass all of the elements of differentiation we have discussed so far (while at the same time retaining the underlying research-based skills). Differentiation may, for example, occur by grouping; here you can give all pupils the same investigation and differentiate by role within the group or by giving different groups different investigations. Further, you might choose to scaffold an investigation, giving some pupils 'hint cards' to support their development and to ensure that they work towards the desired outcome. There is also the option of giving different pupils access to different resources: some may use tablet devices, some texts and images, some video sources and so on. Alternatively, you may allow some pupils to research freely (for example, an open internet search – where they must determine the quality of sources) and others a more structured approach with a selection of recommended sources that they can use to support their investigation. There are endless possibilities for differentiation during an investigation and, while you may immediately think about differentiation by outcome, I urge you to think carefully about the many other options available and integrate them where appropriate to ensure all pupils access the learning and make progress while, at the same time, encouraging independent thinking. It very much depends on the activity itself and the outcomes you are hoping to achieve (beginning with the end in mind) as to how you structure, design and differentiate an investigation. Never underestimate your own role in investigative tasks – any teacher who thinks that pupils 'just get on with it' and then 'see what the outcomes are' will do pupils a disservice. Teachers need to support pupils by giving sufficient guidance and feedback during the process – this allows pupils to develop (a formative approach). It is essential that pupils are very clear on the purpose of the investigation, that they are provided with directions for how to develop the project, and that you circulate within the classroom in order to answer questions and encourage pupil motivation.

Essay-based tasks can also be classed as open-ended. They can be differentiated through, for example, the use of writing frames. Some pupils may be confident to write an essay or develop an assignment unaided yet others require support. For example, an essay requiring pupils to 'outline the trend in UK unemployment from 2001 to 2011, explaining the various causes of unemployment and describing the approaches governments may use to deal with each one'. The more-able pupils may confidently research the topic, be able to highlight key points and then formulate an argued response. The less-able pupils may require sources of information (from which they can select key facts) and possibly a writing frame or prompts. This might include, for example, possible starter sentences for key paragraphs:

- Unemployment is defined as…
- In 2001 employment figures were…
- In 2011 employment figures were…
- The trend in unemployment was…

- The key factors are…
- The governments in power were…
- A government can take the following key steps…

It may be necessary to provide a list of key words that pupils will need to include to ensure they make reference to subject specific vocabulary and terminology. It might also be important to remind pupils that, for each point that they make, they must explain it and provide supporting evidence (perhaps three key sources). A brief reminder sheet may be required for some pupils to support their writing, of the form:

- Key statement made or opinion given (what point are you trying to make – does it link to the question?).
- Explanation of this statement or view (reasoning and justification).
- Key evidence to support this viewpoint (how do you know):
  1)
  2)
  3)
- How does the next paragraph link?

Differentiation by grouping

Differentiation by grouping is a key differentiation strategy and many of the activities we have discussed lend themselves to group work. But how do we group? This is one of the questions I am always asked and it is one that concerns teachers. I worry about why it is a concern. We should only focus on 'how we group' once we are clear on the learning purpose and type of activity that we are using. This will provide us with all of the information we need. It will tell us whether we need to group by mixed ability, learning preference or similar ability. There is, of course, no 'right or wrong' answer and usually teachers are concerned with this when they are being observed. My answer is to be clear on why you are grouping and you will then be able to justify how you group. Any school that insists, for example, on mixed–ability grouping will be missing out on the benefits of all of the other possibilities and we should always mix things up to develop the very best learning in our classrooms.

The main concern for many teachers is not grouping by similar ability (this seems logical and often easy to apply) but when we mix ability. This is an immediate natural concern and the focus then needs to be on how each pupil will benefit from being in the group and the role that they will take. Often teachers worry that the more able will be 'held back' by the less able, thus limiting their progress. In fact the opposite is true because the more able benefit from 'teaching' the less able. In doing this they have to explain and think of different ways of approaching a topic and so they explore different possibilities and deepen their own understanding. A further concern is that the more able will dominate and leave the less able behind – this is where roles and responsibilities in a group become important.

The role pupils take within the group, whether similar or mixed ability, is a form of differentiation. It is important that we rotate the role with future groupings so that all pupils experience the different roles within a group setting. We can allocate roles (if we think a pupil needs to develop a particular area or impact their strength), allow pupils to assign roles within their group or to randomly allocate roles. It very much depends on the context. There are project roles such as leader (taking the role as chair), editor (organising the final product), spokesperson (presents the group's findings), recorder (takes notes and keeps track of resources) and checker (double checks for accuracy), and discussion roles such as timekeeper (keeps a note of timings), facilitator (keeps the discussion moving and focused), reflector (interprets what is being said and summarises, asking the original speaker if the summary is an accurate reflection of what they said), elaborator (makes connections between current discussion and prior learning) and summariser (provides a brief summary at key points for other pupils to agree). There are other roles that you will no doubt use and, whatever you name the specific role, it is important that pupils understand what is expected of them and what they should expect from others in the group. What we don't want is group work to be an opportunity for 'shy' pupils to fall into the background and not contribute. Research suggests that approximately seven per cent of pupils will 'coattail' (Kaufman *et al.*, 1999). We want to avoid this and to use group work as an opportunity to build confidence in learners. As well as the task itself, group processing – where the group reflect on their progress – is an essential part of group work. As part of this process pupils need to:

- **Feedback**: each pupil in the group gives and receives positive feedback on their contribution to the group. The feedback needs to be positive to generate forward momentum towards improving performance.
- **Reflect**: pupils need to be given the opportunity to reflect on the feedback they have been given.
- **Set improvement goals**: pupils and groups need to set targets for improvement – identifying their next steps. This might be a key skill for an individual or future development for the group.
- **Celebrate**: to create a positive culture of learning it is important that each group identifies their successes and that they embrace the positive feedback.

There are various types of group activity and here we consider a few that can be adapted as a basis for new types of activity. The first is the Jigsaw. This can be used in a variety of different ways. Pupils are grouped (for example, red table, blue table, etc.). All of the pupils within a group are given a number (one to five, for example). All of the pupils numbered one form a new group and so on. Pupils gather information in their new groups – they might be using different resources or working on different parts of a problem or learning a new skill or gaining a new vital piece of information to take back to their group (which they must first interpret in their new group and then teach it to their original group). After a period they return to their original groupings where they relay the information and this is pieced together to solve the original problem. The spokesperson from each group can then summarise the groups findings, which can be peer-assessed by the rest of the class. Differentiation here is mainly through the numbering of pupils, and is often by ability. It could be a situation where the coloured tables (red, blue, and so on) have mixed-ability groupings but the numbers we give pupils within these groups (one, two, and so on) will result in new groups where those numbered one will be of a similar ability, those numbered two will be of a similar ability, and so on – this then differentiates the 'numbered' groups by task but all pupils still contribute fully to the overarching task when they return to their original (coloured) group. We might also simply take a purely random mixed-ability approach.

Another type of group activity is where we group by the type of activity – allowing a pupil choice in the resource that they think will best develop their learning. This may mean the use of tablet devices or computers for some, practical activities for others, reading materials and so on. To avoid pupils going where their friends choose, ask them to write their choice in secret and to then go to the table they select. We can add a further dimension of choice through the topic. For example, it may be that you are looking at monarchs through time and pupils choose (or are assigned) to a specific monarch – they need to identify as a group three key points associated with the specific reign. It may be that each group is looking at a different character from a text studied in literature. There are many different possibilities with group activities – the most important thing is to ensure that all pupils benefit and learn from the experience. Group work should develop higher-level thinking skills, interpersonal and communication skills. Another dimension is where individuals in a group play a different role in terms of a character. For example, it might be courtroom drama roles including: perpetrator, judge, three jurors, a prosecutor and a defence barrister. This can link to characters in a text for a given scenario in drama or in literacy. In history pupils may play different characters in a given period such as, for example, in Medieval times where they may re-enact a scene using key criteria and learn about individual roles in society – becoming experts in their role and then teaching others.

When group work is the basis for cooperative learning, it is important to ensure that each pupil understands that their contribution to the group is essential (in other words if one piece of the jigsaw is missing it can't be completed). Cooperative learning contains the following:

- positive interdependence – every role is important – we succeed or fail together;
- individual and group accountability;
- face-to-face interaction;
- explicit learning of interpersonal and team work skills;
- group processing – evaluating team functioning.

Individual learning preferences

We stray into a minefield if we try to classify learners as fixed visual, auditory or kinaesthetic stereotypes. Although we may have a dominant modality, most argue that we benefit from developing all of our senses to the full. However, it is important, as practitioners, to have an awareness of the different learning preferences and the ways in which different activities can be designed to support these. This allows us to implement variety in our lessons and to develop a more engaging learning environment. After all, our environment is multi-sensory and so we should include this in the learning experience.

Visual learners prefer to use images, photographs, diagrams, maps, colours and so on to communicate and to organise information. They learn best by processing and relaying learning in this way. They enjoy board games, picture games and reading games and the visual aid to learning provided when we use an interactive whiteboard. You will often find that they synthesise learning using mind maps or diagrams.

Auditory learners are those who benefit from listening to explanations, instructions and who prefer to provide verbal explanations. They enjoy language games that are mainly listening-based, including those that involve repetition, dictation and listening for clues. They benefit from activities that are group-based and involve discussion (peer hearing and active contribution).

Kinaesthetic learners are those who learn best by 'doing'. They enjoy activities that involve them moving or physically moving objects, such as card sorts, interactive whiteboard activities, game-based learning, making things and drama and role play. They will struggle in a rigid learning environment that forces one particular style.

Teaching assistants

Teaching assistants support learners in our classrooms and are trained in this respect. They are an obvious way in which we differentiate support in our lessons. A problem that is frequently encountered is that there is insufficient liaison between the class teacher and the teaching assistant prior to the lesson. In other words, the teaching assistant goes to the lesson 'blind' – they have not been prepared to support learning in the classroom. If we are to maximise the impact of teaching assistants in our classrooms then we must make time to discuss with them the learning that will be visited in the lesson and, most importantly, the ways in which they can support learners or the specific learner with whom they work. This means that teaching assistants have the opportunity to engage in discussion with you about the type of support they offer and to ensure that they develop learning in the correct way (we want to avoid teaching assistants having to try to interpret the lesson during the lesson as this can lead to misconceptions for pupils). Therefore, the very best way to differentiate learning with the support of a teaching assistant is to liaise with them before the lesson and ensure they are confident with the concepts and process to be developed and used in the lesson, and that they can access the resources and techniques to support learning in the best possible way.

Cross-curricular collaboration

If our aim is to create learners who can apply their skills and knowledge in different contexts, and who can make connections between subjects and indeed areas within an individual subject, then we will most likely create much more rounded individuals who continue confidently to the world of work or higher education. In order to achieve this there does need to be a consistent approach to learning. For example, if physics and mathematics use different methods to rearrange formulae then all we do is divorce one from the other. Pupils cannot make the connection and they get confused with the number of different approaches they are expected to learn. In reality this comes down to teachers requiring training, more so than schools having a policy for numeracy across the curriculum or whole school literacy. Teachers need to see this in action.

One of the ways to make these connections is through cross-curricular collaboration or projects. These are more than the off-curriculum day often timetabled into the academic programme for the year – they are a theme that may run over the course of a half term or a few weeks. It may be a source simply for home learning – a termly theme that subjects agree on. What is important is that we allow all pupils to access the work and, in working jointly on a project, teachers benefit from communicating with each other and this may be communication about ideas for differentiation, classroom management, and so on. It may even lead to them observing parts of each other's lesson or, where the timetable allows, team teaching. The theme might be something as simple as 'trees'. A mathematics lesson might focus on symmetry of leaves or circumference of tree trunks, in biology the different conditions in which different trees flourish, in DT different sources of wood and their uses, and so on – the list is endless. The key is in ensuring that all staff embed the theme into their lessons and that pupils are encouraged to apply their learning.

For a targeted collaborative approach where teachers work much more closely together an example would be something like recipes (Bartlett, 2015). Recipes provide a wonderful cross curricular opportunity. MFL can introduce the recipe in a target language (one language if all pupils study a single language). Pupils can be asked to translate the recipe or to answer a series of questions (you may use different recipes for different groups of students through discussion with DT, mathematics and MFL). In mathematics you can study ratio and pupils can be asked to develop the recipe for different servings so that, for example, they re-write a 'serves 8' recipe as a 'serves 12' recipe. The assessment focus here is on the technique and method that pupils use (can they effectively use the unitary method?). This may only be a short plenary task as part of a lesson developing the concept of ratio and need not take up substantial lesson time. For an extension pupils can be asked to explain the mathematical process. When pupils make the product in DT, assessment is in both the 'how' (i.e. during the process) and in the quality of the final product (there could be a tasting similar to Masterchef (www.bbc.co.uk) where pupils present their product), with explicit assessment criteria to support pupils in assessing their own progress and perhaps for redirecting them. There are lots of different avenues to this very simple project. A continuance would be designing packaging for the product and developing a marketing campaign (this can be in English and also in the modern foreign language used) with links to ICT or business studies. None of these activities are particularly onerous on individual subjects and all demonstrate progress in learning across a range of subjects in a rather simple but very effective way. It also embraces all types of learners and allows everyone to access the curriculum. Equally, it could of course form an extended cross curricular home-learning project.

Summary

Learning, in the main, is typically where we develop concepts and embed learning. These stages of the learning cycle are usually longer in this phase. It is important to remember, however, that all four phases must still be experienced in order to secure high impact learning (as discussed in Chapter 2). Figure 4.5 demonstrates a single or parallel sequence of learning cycles. Activities during the main part of the lesson can be differentiated in a number of ways and pupils are involved in developing their own learning pathway. The key is to be clear on what you want pupils to achieve and then thinking about how they are going to get there, encompassing all of the various learning needs but doing so in a manageable and beneficial way. Maintaining this focus in the planning stage will support differentiation for learning.

During the main part of the lesson:

*   Are you clear on the learning purpose of each activity?
*   Will it support pupils in working towards the learning outcomes? How?
*   What are the success criteria?
*   Does the activity need to be differentiated?

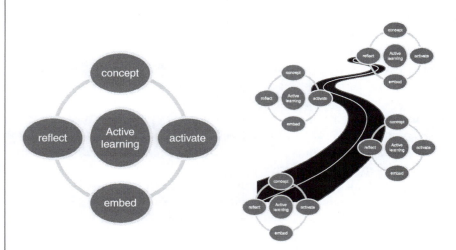

Figure 4.5 The learning cycle, and possible sequence of learning cycles within the main part of the lesson, to illustrate that learning is not always a smooth journey but can take many twists and turns.

- How will differentiation best support learning?
- Do you use a variety of resources to ensure all pupils experience different learning styles?
- Do the activities engage pupils?
- Are all pupils able to access the activity and do they know what is expected of them?
- How will you assess progress and use this to guide next steps?
- Are pupils involved in this process and to what extent is pupil choice observed?
- Have pupils experienced all four stages of the learning cycle (albeit for different durations)?
- Have you discussed learning in the lesson with any teaching assistants?

Differentiation for learning: the final challenge

The end of the lesson is often referred to as the plenary. It typically constitutes 20 to 25 per cent of the lesson and is a period that should further challenge learning, offering the opportunity for self-evaluation and reflection. This consolidation provides further formative evidence to inform future planning. It is therefore very important to allow sufficient time for the plenary as it is a key part of the learning process. Unfortunately, teachers very often rush the plenary or they run out of time (skipping it completely). It is not a case of making it a discrete part of the lesson (pens down we are now doing the plenary) but one that transitions smoothly from learning in the main body of the lesson and adds that extra dimension to learning, placing more emphasis on reflection and review in the learning cycle, and further enhancing thinking skills. The plenary is also an opportunity for pupils to revisit the Big Question and to determine whether they have made progress (remember that an outstanding lesson should demonstrate progress for all pupils). The Big Question provides tangible evidence of progress and, if styled correctly, it will support pupils in thinking about whether they have met the learning outcomes for the lesson and in identifying any areas that require further development. Different types of activity lend themselves best to this phase of the lesson, rather than perhaps the start or main body of the lesson, simply because of the learning purpose, although it is important not to stick to any one particular type of activity and to mix it up. In this chapter we outline activities that tend to work well as plenaries and identify opportunities for differentiation.

The Big Question

Returning to the Big Question is essential. If we simply run out of time then the activity loses its learning purpose and has no value (the value is in high quality comparison). So always ensure that you allow sufficient time to revisit and develop the question further. In some cases the Big Question may form the plenary activity itself and on other occasions it may be returned to for a brief period (for example, two minutes). It is used to identify progress and as a platform for assessing learning in the lesson – this can be self-, peer- or teacher-assessment. There is undeniably great learning value in asking pupils to compare their answer at the start of the lesson to their answer at the end of the lesson. It not only provides tangible evidence of progress but it encourages pupils to think: what have they learned in the lesson? How do they know this? Have they developed their subject-specific language? What do the words mean and how do they apply to the specific context? Did they have any prior misconceptions? Can they now explain these? Why did their answer change? How did their thinking develop? What processes have they used? What are the key concepts? The questions and possibilities are endless but the underlying process is that we are developing pupils' thinking skills and their ability to reflect: pupils leave the lesson with a sense of having achieved. While we want all pupils to make progress, that progress may be at varying rates; remember that no matter how small, progress is progress and we must celebrate success if we are to create an environment that promotes learning and pupil engagement.

At this point it is worth mentioning plenaries such as 'what have you learned today', which are common practice as a model of reflection. If you use this technique then take a moment to reflect on its purpose. How do you use it? How do pupils use it? Does it inform your planning? Is it a meaningful activity that impacts on and deepens learning? What is the learning purpose? Is this achieved? In reality what happens is that pupils attempt to regurgitate the learning outcomes. They write down anything that they think will satisfy the teacher, and the teacher in turn is most likely doing this to satisfy an outdated teaching and learning or assessment policy or to 'pass' a marking audit. If we are honest with ourselves, how often do we use what pupils write to inform future planning? We probably don't since most teachers do not have the opportunity to read these books immediately after the lesson in sufficient time for planning the following lesson. Therefore, I urge you to use the Big Question as discussed above as a platform for this type of self-assessment. A carefully crafted and well thought out Big Question will clearly demonstrate what 'pupils have learnt' in the context of a learning challenge and it is far more meaningful to compare their initial and final responses to inform your planning (this can be through observation or marked work – stick the initial and final responses in the pupils' books). These are sample extracts taken from actual pupil responses to Big Questions:

1) Can a flame change colour?

   Initial response: 'No'.

   Final response: 'A flame can change colour depending on what we put in it. We used different metals and the flames changed colour. Some went purple. The colour it burns tells you which metal it is'.

   Initial response: 'Not sure – they might be different shades of orange'.

   Final response: 'When we heat metals in a flame they change its colour. Potassium went purple and copper a greeny-blue. If we want to check what metal something is we can use the flame test. The colour it burns tells us what metal it is. We can also use it to confirm the results of a precipitate test. Something with copper in it will burn greeny-blue.'

These responses tell us that pupils are aware that flames can change colour and when we might use this. The second pupil gives an example of how this might be applied in practice.

2) I take the same amount of sodium chloride and silver chloride – will they both dissolve in water?

Initial response: 'Yes. Both are same name and sodium chloride is salt and this dissolves so silver chloride should do the same'.

Final response: 'Silver chloride is insoluble and this is the same as lead chloride'.

Initial response: 'No idea'.

Final response: 'No. Sodium chloride dissolves and is soluble but silver chloride is insoluble'.

In these responses, while there is no explanation, pupils are using the correct terminology (soluble and insoluble) and have provided an additional example.

3) A rectangle has sides $(2a + 1)$ and $(3a − 2)$. What is its area?

Initial response: '$5a − 1$'.

Final response: '$(2a + 1) \times (3a− 2) = 2a(3a − 2) + 1(3a −2) = 6a^2 − 4a + 3a −2 = 6a^2 − a − 2$'.

Initial response: '$(2a + 1) \times (3a − 2) = 6a − 2$'.

Final response: 'Rectangle method (pupil had demonstrated this) to give $6a^2 − 1a − 2$'.

These responses would give rise to the opportunity to discuss the different methods used, notation (for example, a or $1a$) and collection of like terms.

4) Do plants need light?

Initial response: 'No. Plants don't need light like we do because they don't have eyes and don't need to see'.

Final response: 'Plants need light to make food for themselves. The more light they get the faster they make food. The food is called glucose and they use carbon dioxide and water and light to make glucose and oxygen. The oxygen is needed for animals to live'.

Initial response: 'Plants are fine in the dark'.

Final response: 'Plants need light for photosynthesis which is the process of making food and oxygen from carbon dioxide. This food helps plants to grow. Plants also need other minerals. If there is no light it limits the rate of photosynthesis. Light is absorbed by chlorophyll. We need the oxygen to survive and so do animals. More light increases the rate of photosynthesis. So yes plants need light to grow and we need them to grow to produce oxygen.'.

In this example we can see that both pupils have significantly developed their responses and used scientific language to explain the process and why it is important. In this case the pupils have clearly developed their learning and are able to articulate this, demonstrating their progress.

We have discussed the use of the Big Question and now we need to turn our attention to differentiation. Owing to the nature of this activity and because we use it to create a comparative response, it is important that it is designed to encompass the key learning outcomes. In many respects one could argue that if all pupils are given the same question then differentiation is by outcome. Therefore, to create more specific and targeted differentiation opportunities, give pupils or groups of pupils different Big Questions. They should really all allow open development of learning (i.e. not apply a glass ceiling and limit progress) but may be worded differently, scaffolding may be used to support learning when you return to the question (based on pupil performance during the lesson – assessment to inform differentiation), or it may simply be a question that involves application using other elements of prior learning that need to be developed or embedded. All of these are examples of targeted differentiation and can be adapted with ease. An additional use can be to use post-it notes where pupils post their initial response at the start of the lesson and, as the lesson progresses and they want to add to their response, they can do so on a different coloured post-it note (you may allocate a one-minute period for this part at a key point in the lesson) and then, at the end of the lesson, post their final response on a different coloured post-it note. This creates a situation where we develop learning in progress – almost like a learning story. It is quite a powerful technique and one to use as a tool on occasion. Pupils can either use it to discuss their learning journey or, alternatively, you might pick some interesting examples for discussion (this relies on having a safe learning environment).

If you use the Big Question as a team activity then, again, this can be differentiated in a number of ways. It could be that all groups are given the same Big Question or that different groups are given different Big Questions. When teams re-group at the end of the lesson then it is important that they enter into meaningful learning discussions. They must focus on providing supporting evidence for their revised answer, focusing on key points developed during the lesson. Differentiation by grouping was discussed in Chapter 4 and the techniques outlined there can be used here. Typically though, when we give groups a Big Question to work on, we would make this activity the plenary activity itself.

Plenary activities

An outstanding plenary should allow pupils to make connections in their learning, allow for metacognition and encourage independence, debate and discussion. It should challenge pupils and assess the progress that they have made during the lesson. All pupils should be able to access the plenary and, while this may be at different levels, it is important that we do not apply a glass ceiling through the activity but allow open development. The plenary should not be more of the same and should build further challenge and reflection into the lesson, offering a different application of skills, knowledge and understanding and demonstrating further progress in learning. Some teachers use past exam questions in the plenary (particularly for exam groups) and there is no reason past exam questions should not be used as long as they offer a different challenge to those used in the lesson. Try to select an example that combines different techniques or knowledge from combined topics.

A common feature of plenary activities is that they allow simultaneous whole class assessment and this is why you often see mini-whiteboards (or laminated A4 card as an alternative) being used. Teachers ask a question and pupils 'reveal' their answers (make sure they don't show their answers until you say 'reveal'). While all pupils are completing the same question the power in this activity comes from your use of targeted questions and this will form the basketball-style questioning that stems from each whole class question. This is where differentiation comes into its own and allows you to really probe learning and address any misconceptions. Tablet devices that connect to the interactive whiteboard (for example, iPads using Apple TV) can also be used here – useful as you can display a pupil's individual answer so that this can be discussed in a forum debate. In this section we discuss different plenary activities and potential opportunities for differentiation.

Correcting a response

In this type of activity pupils are asked to correct a response or to compare two or more different responses. This promotes higher-order thinking skills. It is often used if the purpose is for pupils to identify misconceptions and/or to determine whether a particular learning outcome has been achieved. In order to correct a response pupils have to have a good understanding of the 'why' and the 'why not'. This can of course be differentiated by giving different pupils different responses to compare – these can be of differing levels of challenge (ability levels). It is also a good opportunity to encourage pupils to choose (perhaps with your guidance), based upon assessment during the lesson, a response to correct or compare based upon an area that they need to further develop. This is also a good team activity. However, if you do this then it is more difficult, due to time constraints, to discuss collectively as a whole class and so assessment comes through your observation when interacting with or observing the groups. It does work particularly well in groups as a round-robin exercise where each team (keep them small – perhaps three or four pupils in each – to ensure all pupils contribute) has a different coloured pen and they circulate around the room with one minute on each problem adding to the other team's responses. This means pupils are assessing peer responses and then having to develop the answer further or contribute something different. Alternatively, if you use this activity as a single question directed at the whole class (using mini-whiteboards), where you place a question and response on the board and pupils have to correct the response (or comment on it), then ensure that you target questioning and allow sufficient time to highlight the key learning points and that all pupils contribute.

Voting activities

You have no doubt used voting activities during your teaching career but I urge you to take a moment to think about how you have used them in your lessons – what you did with them and why, how they enhanced learning and how they benefitted all pupils. Voting activities are where pupils have to make a choice in response to a particular question and ABCD cards or electronic voting mechanisms are often used. The type of question you ask is extremely important. Dylan Wiliam (Wiliam, 2011) discusses the use of discussion and diagnostic questions in the framework of multiple-choice responses. Discussion questions lead to discussion and 'there is no point in asking this question unless you are going to have the discussion'. Whereas, with diagnostic questions, it would be very unlikely for the pupil to get the correct answer for the wrong reason and therefore you can be confident that if pupils answer correctly they do so because they understand the topic, 'The teacher gains concrete evidence about the students' learning *without* having to have the classroom discussion' (Wiliam, 2011). Diagnostic questions are often used as a quick check of pupil understanding and discussion questions are used when you want to enter into discussions about the reasons for a particular choice (gaining an understanding of pupil thinking). I personally always recommend the use of follow-up questions (when based upon a diagnostic response these may be brief and longer and more thought-provoking for discussion-based questions). It is through this use of questioning that we confirm understanding. Thinking time is also important – pupils have to be allowed sufficient thinking time in order to respond. Therefore careful class management is needed and pupils should only be expected to hold up their A, B, C or D card when you say. By not allowing sufficient thinking time pupils feel rushed. In Chapter 7 we discuss response times to questions and it is useful to implement these techniques here. In terms of differentiation, in this type of activity we ask the whole class the same question to vote on. This means that differentiation occurs through our use of probing questions where we can target and challenge learning at different depths.

The same or different?

This is a comparative activity and, as such, requires pupils to apply their learning – perhaps in a different context. Pupils can compare objects, texts, quotes, images, equations, graphs and so on, identifying one or more similarity and one or more difference. This makes an ideal activity for differentiation as you can tailor the items for comparison according to individual learning needs. This can be directed through formative assessment during the lesson as learning develops and through pupil choice.

It also works nicely as an activity where pupils have to run to one side of the room or the other when they spot a difference or a similarity. They can then be asked to identify these and this can be used as a platform for whole class discussion. Adding a more physical element to the activity just adds a different dimension to learning and makes it more 'fun' for pupils (but not to the detriment of academic content). Odd-one-out activities work in much the same way as before; by making a choice pupils are comparing items and therefore thinking about applying their learning. This can again be used as a more formal task or you can place images around the room and pupils have to go to the odd one out (you might want to ask them to jot it down first before they go so that they aren't influenced by the mass movement of classmates).

What was the question?

This type of activity is extremely powerful – give the whole class a particular answer and ask them to decide what the question was. This naturally differentiates as the quality of the question is usually determined by a pupil's ability and level of understanding (ask them to think of the most challenging question that they can). So, for example, if we have completed a question on rounding to one decimal place and the answer was 3.4 and we ask pupils what the question was, invariably you get a lot of responses (based upon rounding a number to one decimal place). The immediate thought that pupils have is that the number they rounded was 3.42, 3.44 (a simple initial response) and so on and some (usually the more able) might extend this to 3.4123 or 3.4421356. Only a few will offer answers on the other side of the spectrum such as, for example, 3.35621. Questioning can be used to probe understanding and to extend pupils' thinking – challenging their choice – providing further opportunity for differentiation. In biology, during a lesson on photosynthesis, simple word answers may be used like, for example, oxygen, carbon dioxide, and so on. Pupils have to decide on the question. This makes for a nice paired activity.

Connections

Placing images or objects around the room or even along a washing line and asking pupils to make the connection is another activity that can involve prior learning or content knowledge in the plenary activity, or involve the application of newly acquired knowledge or skills. It can also be done as a carousel activity where teams compete against each other and, towards the end of the activity, whole-class discussion focuses on the connection – pupils develop their reasoning skills. You can make this as challenging as appropriate. If necessary, prepare hint cards for pupils to look at (although they must keep the coloured sheet to identify that they used the hint to support their answer), or provide some groups with a choice of three possibilities to choose from (scaffolding learning).

A further application of 'making connections' can be where we place success criteria or learning outcomes on a washing line. Pupils then have to think of an example from each or they may choose to highlight an area they found challenging and place them along the washing line. Indeed it may be appropriate to encourage pupils to think about how one success criterion builds on or supports another and how they connect the different aspects of learning. This demonstrates the progress individual pupils have made and allows them to really think about how they can evidence this or where they may need further support.

Hidden questions

You will often see (particularly at KS3 and younger) pass–the–parcel activities. This is where a question is either in a hat or box and, when the music is stopped, a pupil has to pull the question out of the hat and then answer it. I would recommend adapting this activity slightly – instead of a single hat circulating, have two. One will contain the questions and the other all of the pupils' names. When the music stops the person with the 'question hat' asks the question to the whole class. After a minute of thinking time, the person with the 'names hat' pulls out the pupil who will respond. This means that all pupils have to listen to the question and think about it – if you simply ask the person who pulls the question out to answer then other pupils tend to switch off as it isn't their turn (put the names back in each time so that even those who have answered a question may still be chosen again – in other words they still have to listen and think). You can obviously springboard questions off their response and differentiate in this way. An alternative to this is to have teams competing against each other – they can pick colour-coded questions according to the level of challenge and earn different points for their team.

Question checkers

If you used an open-ended starter activity to generate a series of questions at the start of the lesson that pupils would like to be able to answer, then the plenary is the opportunity to dedicate time to addressing these questions. The idea (hopefully) being that pupils can now explain and discuss (providing examples) in order to answer the question they had at the start of the lesson. Pick key questions generated from the starter that identify key outcomes. This type of plenary (perhaps used without the Big Question) allows pupils to see very clearly the progress they have made – they are able to answer a question that they could not answer at the start of the lesson and explain their response.

Game-based activities

Game-based activities need to be carefully managed but can work well as a plenary activity – although good time management is essential. 'Guess who' games are often used in, for example, languages where the teacher is reading out a series of clues (for example, clues to describe an animal) and pupils have to identify the item. This can be written down in secret – pupils note down how many clues it took them and then how they arrived at their choice. Similarly this can be done in English where we describe key characteristics of a character in a play or story. Pupils have to identify who it was and, as an extension, any other characteristics they would have highlighted to identify the character more succinctly. It is important to summarise with, for example, three key characteristics or to allow pupils to assess the characteristics they identified with three that you have chosen. This encourages pupils to compare and contrast and to enter into debate. Other games of this nature include The LOGO board game (http://www.drumondpark.com) where pupils have to describe an image of an item given the logo. This might be a football or flowers or a cereal. The power is in the description that the pupils give and in using it to advance learning. If used in MFL then the key is to determine three descriptive statements that could identify the product. It is equally powerful in a business studies lesson focusing on brand – is the brand easily identifiable? What makes it unique? Is it a powerful summary of the product encapsulated in an image or phrase?

Another popular game used in the classroom is top trumps – one the younger years particularly like. The cards are similar to those issued with new toys or the swap cards that pupils buy. As with all activities, clarifying the learning purpose is key – why does playing the game enhance learning? How do you know? You don't have to prepare this sort of game from scratch. There are many resources online that are already prepared – all you have to do is adapt them to suit the needs of the pupils in your classroom. The one benefit of activities such as top trumps is that they can be very easily differentiated, both through the content of the trump card and also the questions that are asked. Top trumps can be played directly as the game or the cards can be used in reverse to generate questions. Often teachers like to use these in an 'argue your case' activity where pupils respond to a statement given on their card and physically move around the room to create different clusters of information.

Comment-based plenaries

A comment-based plenary is exactly as the name suggests – one where we ask pupils to make comments on learning in the lesson. Taken as a 'what have I learnt' type of activity limits its value (as mentioned before, pupils tend to simply regurgitate learning outcomes). Best practice is to build in thinking and reflection. It is the reflection that will deepen learning. What we need to do is carefully select an activity that promotes reflection; this will produce the best comment-based outcomes. For example, you might ask pupils to write down three headlines to summarise the lesson that include any key vocabulary or terms. This should be expanded with a short example. You might ask them to write a brief summary for a non-subject specialist.

The plenary can also be an opportunity to set the scene for an open task – possibly to be completed for home learning (which we discuss later in this chapter). If this is the case it is an opportunity to generate ideas and to ensure all pupils are clear on the activity (as discussed in Chapter 3). The activities that can be used in the plenary are endless and you can adapt many different styles. What is important is that it challenges learning and it builds in time for reflection.

Reflection

Reflection is an essential component of the learning cycle and, while it occurs at key points during the lesson (as learning develops), there is greater weighting on the reflective thought process in the plenary. By its nature it involves learners thinking about what they have developed during the lesson. What worked well? What didn't work? How have they overcome this? What resources did they use to support them? How have they made progress against learning outcomes? What determines this progress? How do they know? Reflective thought is often an individual exchange between teacher and learner forming a learning dialogue. This can be written or verbal; if a pupils reflects on their learning and records this, as a teacher you need to respond. Pupils then know that there is value in the exercise. If we are honest then we know that if we ask pupils to traffic-light their performance (a RAG rating), indicate with a smiley face or similar, or write down what they have learnt during the lesson, we don't always get the best results (pupils don't really think about the process). Common sense dictates that a pupil could simply indicate they were green without any real understanding, and when pupils are asked to write down what they have learnt often they simply regurgitate the learning outcomes or success criteria without thinking (you will commonly hear 'but what should I write?'). This type of activity alone is rendered meaningless and a waste of valuable learning time. Therefore, it is important that this forms part of the interactive feedback process. The same goes for when we ask a pupil 'did you understand that?' Most will simply say 'yes' (irrespective of whether they did or didn't).

Reflection does not have to be a static activity; I often use progression lines. They allow pupils to relate their learning experience directly to the outcomes for the lesson. Place learning outcomes around the room on different pieces of A3 sugar paper (or use a washing line). For each learning outcome ask pupils to think carefully of an example and to take a post-it note and place it by the specific learning outcomes or success criteria. What this does is encourage pupils to think about the learning outcomes in the context of the lesson (this may seem a silly statement but often pupils find learning outcomes detached from the lesson – something that teachers place up on the board at the start of the lesson). What results is a very powerful learning or progression map (photograph this if you need to record pupil progress) that you can then use to formulate discussion. Pupils can then retrieve their post-it notes and stick them in their books.

Sometimes pupils need support when they are asked to reflect on learning in a lesson and Table 5.1 acts as a useful series of prompts – a guide to remind pupils that for every statement they make they must support this with an example or an explanation that demonstrates understanding.

Table 5.1 Ideas for prompts.

Prompt
I did…well, because I can…An example is….
I need to work on…because….
My learning targets are…so that I can….
How I managed to answer the Big Question….
My next steps in learning are…to achieve…because I want to be able to….
I will know I have been successful because….

Reverse bell work

Bell work is sometimes used at the start of the lesson when pupils' arrival is staggered over a few minutes. This ensures that pupils are engaged with a learning activity from the moment they enter the classroom and the climate for learning is established. Of course, if we were to assess this at the start of the lesson then there is the potential to waste valuable learning time. Therefore, much better practice is to use it at the end of the lesson with the same purpose as at the start: quick-fire questions that ensure pupils are focused at all times. When pupils are packed away, ready to leave, use reverse bell work and return to the question or questions and develop appropriately (keeping it very brief). If you personalised bell work by giving individuals different questions (perhaps five questions distributed to individuals across the class) then ask only quick-fire questions based on these (rather than developing basketball-type questioning from a single question). The idea is to keep these topics as something of which pupils need frequent reminding. In mathematics, for example, this could be the multiplication of positive and negative numbers (reminding pupils of the rules in this way means it tends to become a more natural calculation).

Home learning

Home learning should be personalised in much the same way as we personalise learning in the classroom. If we set all pupils the same task (usually a set of questions) then this is typically set to the middle, which means high-attaining pupils disengage (home learning loses its value and becomes something they complete with ease and quickly) and low-attaining pupils cannot access the activity and struggle (they also disengage). Therefore home learning should be differentiated and pupil choice should be an important part of this process. As I have emphasised before, while we can have a good idea of the ability of pupils it is important we do not pre-assign them to a specific level of home learning. The choice should be based on performance in the lesson on that particular topic. Some pupils can take to different topics with ease and find others very challenging, requiring additional support. If you are preparing home-learning activities then pitch them at three levels and increase autonomy in your classroom by encouraging a climate where pupils take ownership of their learning and the next challenge they take.

Activities that allow all pupils to make progress at their individual rates are research- or investigation-based home-learning activities. These can rely on the acquisition of skills over a period and can be an extended project. Some schools make this cross-curricular and thematic-based and the results are usually positive. Whichever route you take, the very best homework activities encourage pupils to apply and make real-life connections (in other words they are not just more of the same). We have to make it different and interesting for pupils to 'want to do it'. Whether we like it or not there is often a culture of apathy towards home learning but it is an important part of our learning culture and in developing independent study.

Summary

The plenary activity is a time for further challenge along with reflection. Other periods of reflection in the lesson have perhaps been associated with a particular activity but, during the plenary, we must dedicate time to reflecting on learning during the lesson as a whole as a combination of the mini-reflections. It is important that we make time for the plenary and that we ensure that we plan for outstanding learning. The timelines below show different possibilities for structuring the plenary and are based on a 60-minute lesson.

For a challenging Big Question which forms the plenary activity:

- Big Question (seven minutes);
- reflection (five minutes);
- reverse bell work (one minute).

Where the Big Question was simple and only needs a quick response, therefore progress needs to be demonstrated with a plenary activity:

- plenary activity (seven minutes);
- reflection (three minutes);
- Big Question (two minutes);
- reverse bell work (one minute).

No Big Question at all:

- plenary activity (five minutes);
- reflection (three minutes);
- reverse bell work (one minute).

When we plan for an outstanding plenary we must ask ourselves the following questions:

- Can all learners access the plenary activity?
- Does the plenary challenge learning further?

- Does the plenary encourage the use of combined skills and prior learning?
- Have you differentiated the activity?
- How have you differentiated the activity?
- Why have you differentiated the activity?
- Have you returned to the Big Question and allowed sufficient time for pupils to reflect and to compare their initial and final responses?
- Is the Big Question differentiated and, if so, how will you assess progress?
- Does the Big Question determine progress towards the overarching learning outcome for the lesson or series of lessons?
- Have you targeted questioning and asked higher-order questions to reinforce any key concepts?
- Can pupils identify progress in learning?
- Can they identify their next steps?
- How do you/they know?
- At the very end of the lesson have you revisited the bell work?

CHAPTER 6

Assessment for learning and differentiation

Assessment for learning and differentiation go hand in hand to support a personalised approach to learning and to ensure that all pupils make progress. Assessment for learning informs differentiation and differentiation ensures all pupils can access learning. Outstanding teachers use both seamlessly to support teaching and learning in their classrooms. There are two ways in which we assess learning: formative assessment (during the learning process) and summative assessment (usually at the end of a lesson or series of lessons). Formative assessment informs differentiation during the lesson and summative assessment is used to provide information on where to pitch learning. Formative assessment guides learning pathways as learning is taking place (real time) and summative assessment gives us a generalised overview of the level our learners are working at. For example, if we are teaching a class of pupils for whom prior assessment data and targets suggest they are working at grade D overall then we would not begin by pitching a lesson at grade A but, instead, develop learning sensibly and challenge learning to extend thinking. It also provides us with a retrospective view of learning. This chapter does not aim to cover assessment for learning in great depth (it is, after all, a substantial topic in itself and one I have dedicated a book to (Bartlett, 2015)), but to make reference to how it supports differentiation. It is also worth mentioning briefly how we differentiate assessment.

Prior information

Assessment data provides us with a wealth of information and, for some, it can be quite daunting. It is quite simple really – know your pupils. The data alone provides a snapshot of a pupil's academic history or their educational needs. We know from experience that while assessment data tends to provide a good overview it is simply that – an overview. It provides us with an indication of where we should pitch learning and this is particularly useful if we are new to a class. It also indicates to us areas of strength and weakness (for example, if it provides a question-by-question analysis or topic summaries). The best use of pupil data is when it is combined with professional knowledge. Of course one thing to always bear in mind is that this all depends on the quality of the data, and the quality of the data is fully dependent on the quality of the assessments. How reliable is the assessment data? Does it provide a true indicator of a pupil's performance? Does it reflect and correlate to grades on a national level? Are assessments moderated? By whom are the assessments moderated – are they trained? Is marking moderated? Does an analysis of historical data suggest that the data is accurate? These are but a few questions we must ask ourselves before we rely too heavily on data alone as a marker for where to pitch learning or in identifying specific academic needs. However, data will always be a large part of educational practice and our job is to use it to inform our planning, combined with as many other sources of information as possible. Differentiation, assessment and data (not simply quantitative but also qualitative data) piece together to inform learning and the quality of one impacts on the quality of another, as illustrated in Figure 6.1.

Target grades are another source of data. Often pupils are 'set' according to their target grade or 'expected' performance (therefore we are differentiating before we have even taught or perhaps met a pupil – a little early one could argue?). They are typically generated by external sources such as Fischer Family Trust (FFT) or RaiseOnline. Target grades arise from a complex mathematical algorithm that generates forward estimates (often five years ahead – although it is worth noting that estimates are updated each year to reflect progress nationally) based on a pupil's attainment in a 'test' at a given age, which is used along with other factors such as month of birth, gender and socioeconomic parameters. The purpose here is not to discuss target grades (I guide you to Bartlett (2015) for this purpose) but to think carefully about how we use them in the field of differentiation. Target grades are too often over-used by teachers. This is perhaps because we have an examination and

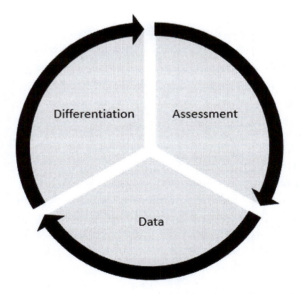

Figure 6.1 Data, assessment and differentiation all piece together to enhance learning. The quality of one impacts on the quality of another.

target-based culture. We must be aware that in some circumstances they can serve to limit progress. If, for example, a pupil has a target grade of E and we use this information to only ever set them work around this level then we limit their potential progress and certainly their ability to achieve a grade C (they aim low because the expectation is low). The reality is that some teachers tend only to expose pupils with lower target grades to lower-ability work and this can lead to disengagement. Some pupils adopt an attitude of 'if I'm not going to get a C what's the point' and low-level behavioural problems can creep in. It is much better to use a target range and all models now have a percentage chance (or likelihood) model that shows the probability of the individual achieving each grade – take this with a pinch of salt because, of course, it is based on the prior performance of similar pupils in similar contexts (if we use contextualised data, which most schools do, such as, for example, FFT D). It does, however, provide you with much more information (and the pupil with increased motivation) on a pupil's potential. If the grade spectrum suggests a target of grade E to C then teachers naturally start to expand the level of work to which they expose pupils (this of course is something we should do anyway, but it does not always happen). In addition we raise expectations. We encourage pupils to aim high. We don't apply a glass ceiling. This increases engagement. Remember, as I keep emphasising, data is no substitute for your professional judgement and for knowing your pupils, so always proceed with caution if relying too heavily on target grades as the main source of information. Figure 6.2 is an example of a percentage chance table. It demonstrates that if we took the most likely grade alone for science, for example, the pupil would have a target grade of C. However, looking closely at the table we can see that the same pupil has an 86 per cent chance of achieving a grade C or above (based on the prior performance of pupils). In other words, think of it rather simply: of those pupils 'similar' to pupil X in terms of their contextualised input data, if what happened last year in examinations is mirrored this year, then the most likely outcomes are that 11 per cent may achieve a grade D, 38 per cent a grade C, 33 per cent a grade B, and so on. Note that 'similar' is based on gender, birth month, previous national tests and teacher assessments – schools have the option to include or exclude the context of their school. When we begin to look at data in this way we naturally raise expectations. If we only consider this pupil as a 'target grade C' (labelled by data) then we would most definitely limit their progress – look closely at the data because it tells you so much more than a single target grade and

Pupil X	KS2 Test			EST	Subject	% chance of achieving KS4 grade							
KS	EN	MA	SC	Basis	Group	G	F	E	D	C	B	A	A*
2	4.9	4.6	5.2	SE	English	1%	1%	2%	12%	35%	34%	14%	2%
2	4.9	4.6	5.2	SE	History	1%	2%	6%	14%	25%	30%	19%	4%
2	4.9	4.6	5.2	SE	ICT	1%	3%	7%	16%	32%	25%	13%	3%
2	4.9	4.6	5.2	SE	Maths	1%	1%	3%	16%	38%	33%	7%	1%
2	4.9	4.6	5.2	SE	MFL	1%	3%	9%	23%	34%	18%	9%	3%
2	4.9	4.6	5.2	SE	Science	1%	1%	2%	11%	38%	33%	13%	2%

Figure 6.2 An example of a grade distribution.

no one pupil is the same. A pupil with a target grade of C, for example, may be more weighted to the lower grades than another pupil. All stakeholders should have access to the likelihood tables and, as a teacher, you most certainly should have seen these for all of your pupils.

Data also provides us with an indication of any special educational needs and this is something that we should all be aware of as teachers. We need to know the needs of our pupils. But it goes beyond this. We need to liaise with the special needs department, learning support assistants, teaching assistants and parents to determine how we can best support the individual in the classroom. This is, of course, where we will differentiate our teaching to ensure that the pupil makes maximum progress and that all those involved are aware of the best possible way in which we can support learning (and importantly continue to liaise with one another). Understanding a pupil's needs and making work accessible for them can ensure that they are able to achieve. I cannot emphasise the importance of liaison enough – despite categorising special educational needs, we cannot categorise the individual. Special educational needs is an expert area and I do not intend to delve into any specifics here, other than to say that there are specialists in your school, such as the SENCO, who will be able to offer a wealth of advice and provide you with materials to read and apply (and a history of what has worked well with the individual pupil to date). The SENCO will support you in differentiating resources or activities to ensure that the individual pupil makes progress and can enjoy and engage fully with the learning process. This is so important if we are to make all learners feel valued and supported, because there is nothing worse for a pupil than being left on the outside or being made to feel like they are 'not good enough'. Making learning inclusive is something that must be more than a 'phrase on paper'. As a little aside, many teachers quote 'time' or lack of it as an excuse for not liaising effectively with the learning support department or parents. I argue that investment initially in this process can save you time in the long run and can make for a happy and productive learning environment.

Which pathway?

Assessment for learning is an on-going process and happens minute-by-minute in lessons whether through observation, discussion, questioning or other medium. Sometimes it forms part of a more formal process (mini-assessments) and these are used to direct learning pathways. We have discussed mini-assessments in Chapters 3, 4 and 5 as part of the lesson planning process and here we look at how the outcome of these are used to map an individual pupil's next steps.

Let us consider a simplified example from mathematics. During a lesson on expanding a single term over a bracket pupils have developed a method based on expanding expressions of the form $a(bx + c)$. Following the development of key concepts, a brief mini-assessment consists of diagnostic questions that highlight different but specific areas (the whole class would attempt these on mini-whiteboards to allow whole-class simultaneous assessment and you would most likely target a few key questions to confirm understanding):

1) $3(2x + 4)$;
2) $5(7 - 4b)$;
3) $-7(8a - 6)$;
4) $3a(4a + 7)$;
5) $6(2x + 1) - 3(2x - 6)$.

As a result of this mini-assessment, some pupils may be confident with all five questions and so would next attempt a more challenging activity. There is absolutely no point in giving these pupils a worksheet that comprises more of the same. If they are confident in all areas then they need further challenge and this should come through applied questions (otherwise learning is static). If a pupil can confidently answer questions 1 to 3 but not 4 or 5 then this tells you that they are able to deal with single terms and with positive and negative numbers. Their area for development is where we have expressions that involve, for example, $a \times a$ and the collection of like terms. A worksheet tailored to this group of pupils may first have a series of questions that involve practising this, leading to questions that involve combining skills and then applying learning. For a pupil who is confident with questions 1 to 4 but struggled on question 5 then it may be that you have a worksheet that focuses initially on collecting like terms and then develops quickly to applied questions. This would involve questions such as $5a + 6b - 3a - 15b$. For pupils who are not confident with multiplying positive and negative numbers then you would support learning with a multiplication grid and a reminder of the rules of multiplication. What is important is that we do not 'stop' learning at what the mini-assessments would imply is a ceiling. We must allow all pupils to access applied questions, while recognising that some may need to be less challenging than others or, alternatively, some may need scaffolding. The information gained from the mini-assessment must only be one source used to plan next steps. For instance, if you simply went on the mini-assessment alone and a pupil whom you had observed to be confident with questions of type 5 but they made a silly mistake, then they would be allocated the wrong pathway and would not make the expected progress. Therefore it is essential to use your knowledge, information from observing learning during the lesson so far, and targeted probing questions following each of the mini-assessment questions to have a clear picture of where learners are, and learners themselves must be confident to articulate that they agree with that pathway (they must be involved in the choice). They need to have an awareness of whether they made a 'silly mistake' in the mini-assessment; in other words if you ask them if they can identify their mistake and correct it then they are able to do so. The main point to be made here is that we are differentiating based upon the outcomes of the lesson so far and the mini-assessment confirms our and the pupil's judgement. This information all combined is the very best way to inform learning. Figures 6.3, 6.4, 6.5 and 6.6 show examples of extracts from possible worksheets that

Linear expansion

Fill in the gaps:

A)

	5b	2
4	20b	

B)

	3a	5
7		

C)

	8y	2
6		

D)

	10 x	6
2		

E)

	9m	−3
5		−15

F)

	6h	−4
3		

Figure 6.3 An example of a worksheet for those requiring additional support.

could be used as a result of the mini-assessment we have discussed. Figure 6.3 is a worksheet that targets those who are struggling with the concept of basic expansion using the rectangle method and who need further support before progressing per-haps to Figure 6.4, which extends learning further (of course some pupils may not progress to Figure 6.4 or may be asked to select the applied questions, for example). Figures 6.5 and 6.6 show worksheets that would target the middle body of learners and the more-able learners respectively. Both give pupils access to applied questions and pupils can self-select the questions from Part A and Part B respectively depending on their levels of confidence. The level of challenge is extended in Figure 6.6. Note that some might say 'why don't we just use a single worksheet that gets progressively more challenging and pupils can start at different points'. The reason for not doing this is that you will have those pupils who need to focus on the early questions never reaching an applied question (time factors) and those who start towards the end find-ing it far too easy and disengaging (there is also, of course, the problem with 'fitting' it all onto one sheet to ensure that we allow the less able to complete the questions they need to support learning and the more able the appropriate challenging questions). We need to challenge all learners and ensure all learners experience the applied ques-tions (that typically come towards the end). Also consider that those who are less able may be very disheartened if all of the questions are on one sheet and they are never able to access certain questions. Remember that they will attempt applied questions at a level of challenge that is appropriate for them (with or without scaffolding) but they will all have the opportunity and be expected to be able to apply their skills. Tailoring worksheets in this way means that we create a culture where all pupils make progress and experience success.

Linear expansion

Expand the following, **showing all working:**

Part A (use the method you are confident with)

1) 3 (a + 2) = __a + 6   2) 4 (y − 2) = __y - __
3) 7 (b − 1) = 7__ - __   4) 2 (b − 7) = __ - __
5) 2 (x + 1)   8) 2 (3 + 2x)
7) 2 (3x − 4)   8) - 3 (2 − 2y)
9) 3 (2a + 9)   10) - 7 (2b − 3)
11) -5 (2p + 3)   12) 2 (3 + 2m)
13) 3 (10 − 2d)   14) 10 (-4b − 3)

Kate says that "3(2a + 4) = 6a + 4" ...is she correct?

Part B

Expand the brackets and collect the like terms:

1) 3 (b − 1) + 4 (b + 2) = 3b - __ + __b + 8 = __b + __

2) 5 (n + 3) − 3 (n + 3) = __n + 15 - __n __ 9 = __n + __

3) 4 (m + 5) + 2 (3m − 5)

4) 3 (2b + 1) − 4 (b + 3)

5) 10 (4b − 3) − 5 (2b − 20)

Part C

1) How would you find the area of the rectangle?

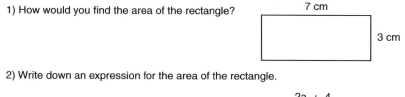

7 cm

3 cm

2) Write down an expression for the area of the rectangle.

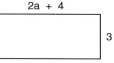

2a + 4

3

3) Can you use the skills above to expand this expression?

Figure 6.4 An example of a worksheet for the less able.

One further point to note in doing this is that all pupils will have achieved the learning outcome for the lesson (perhaps this is, for example, 'to be able to develop a method to multiply a single term over a bracket and apply this to questions in context'). However, they will have done so at different depths. It is the success criteria that map the progression ladder or the depth of learning, but the overarching

Linear expansion

Expand the following, **showing all working**:

Part A

1) 3 (2a + 9)

2) - 7 (2b – 3)

3) -5 (2p + 3)

4) 2 (3 + 2m)

5) 3 (10 – 2d)

6) 10 (- 4b – 3)

7) -5 (2a – 3)

8) -5 (-7 – 5m)

Heidi says that " -7(4b-5) = -28b – 36"…is she correct?

Part B

Simplify the following expressions (expand the brackets and collect the like terms):

1) 3 (b – 1) + 4 (b + 2)

2) 5 (n + 3) – 3(n + 3)

3) 4 (m + 5) + 2 (3m – 5)

4) 3 (2b + 1) – 4 (b + 3)

5) -6 (2b + 4) – 5 (3b -6)

6) -4(-2a – 3) + 4(3a – 7)

Part C

1) Write an expression for the area of the rectangle.

2) Can you simplify this using the skills above?

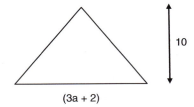

3) How do we find the area of a triangle?

4) Write an expression for the area of the triangle and then expand this expression.

10

(3a + 2)

Figure 6.5 An example of a worksheet for the main body of pupils.

learning outcome offers a generic overview of learning in the lesson and is something that all pupils should be able to achieve (albeit at different levels).

One other aspect of this type of differentiation is the method that pupils feel confident using and applying. One of the underlying principles of differentiation is that we are all different: we are individuals. We all think and process things differently and, therefore, when we expose pupils to something new and we develop concepts we must be aware of the many different ways in which we can approach learning. When

Linear expansion

Expand the following, **showing all working:**

Part A

1) 3 (2a + 9)

2) -7 (2b – 3)

3) -5 (2p + 3)

4) 2 (3 + 2m)

5) 3 (10 – 2d)

6) 10 (-4b – 3)

7) -5 (2a – 3)

8) -5 (-7 – 5m)

Heidi says that "-7 (4b-5) = -28b – 36"...is she correct?

Part B

Simplify the following expressions (expand the brackets and collect the like terms):

1) 3 (b – 1) + 4 (b + 2)

2) 5 (n + 3) – 3 (n + 3)

3) 4 (m + 5) + 2 (3m – 5)

4) 3 (2b + 1) – 4 (b + 3)

5) -6 (2b + 4) – 5 (3b -6)

6) -4 (-2a – 3) + 4 (3a – 7)

Part C

1) Write an expression for:
    a. the perimeter of the rectangle
    b. the area of the rectangle

 7

2) If the length of a rectangle is 8b + 7 and the width is 5, write an expression for the area.

3) If the area of a rectangle is 12y + 8 write down possible expressions for the length and width.

4) Write an expression for the area of triangles A and B (expand both expressions). If a = 4 which triangle is the smallest?

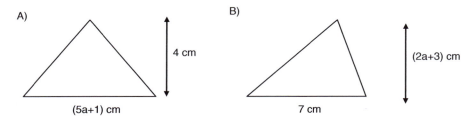

A)   4 cm   (5a+1) cm

B)   (2a+3) cm   7 cm

Figure 6.6 An example of a worksheet for the more able.

teachers opt for the lecture style of teaching, where they demonstrate, illustrate a few examples and then pupils attempt to follow the taught recipe, it means all pupils are exposed to one method – the same method. In these circumstance a teacher will then only resort to discussing another method if pupils simply 'can't get' the first

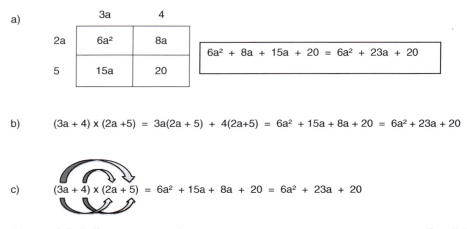

a)

	3a	4
2a	6a²	8a
5	15a	20

6a² + 8a + 15a + 20 = 6a² + 23a + 20

b)   (3a + 4) x (2a +5) = 3a(2a + 5) + 4(2a+5) = 6a² + 15a + 8a + 20 = 6a² + 23a + 20

c)   (3a + 4) x (2a + 5) = 6a² + 15a + 8a + 20 = 6a² + 23a + 20

Figure 6.7 Different ways of approaching the same question: expand $(3a+4)(2a+5)$. Each method is subtly different in the way pupils synthesise and process the question; it is important that we expose pupils to the different methods so that they gain optimum understanding, can 'think' independently and explain the 'why'.

method. This means that we impose instruction on pupils. In contrast, when we use concept development or develop learning though investigation or questioning then we promote thinking skills and understanding. Pupils may naturally develop a particular method and other pupils a different one dependent upon how they approach a question. The one that best suits their learning. As long as the different methods are robust and of sound subject then pupils can use the method that they are most comfortable with. Essentially we allow choice in learning. This is an example of differentiation and one that learners themselves develop (creating autonomy). Figure 6.7 shows different methods for expanding two brackets that pupils naturally differentiate by experience and choice (in this case by prior experience with number and by how they visualise the question). It is important to encourage this choice and allow pupils to direct their own learning. All of the methods are of a sound mathematical nature and so, as a teacher, we are happy that in any one lesson pupils may be using different techniques to answer the same question; pupils are using the technique they are most confident with, that allows them to access the learning and that will maximise their progress. Most importantly, the technique is one that they understand and, because of this understanding, can then apply.

Marking and feedback

Marking and feedback form an essential part of the assessment for learning process and they inform our future planning and pupils' future learning (differentiated pathways). Of course for it to have any impact at all marking needs to be timely and used at key points in a sequence or series of lessons. Marking a piece of work two weeks down the line is absolutely pointless and loses its purpose. That being said, it is unrealistic to expect a teacher to mark every piece of work (especially when a school's assessment for learning policy dictates marking to be in a specific and often lengthy way). Teachers in secondary education potentially teach five classes of 30 pupils on a given day – that's 150 books to assess every day if we marked every piece of work. Primary teachers may cover five different curriculum areas with a class of 30 pupils during a day – that's 150 pieces of work to mark. This of course is not possible and should not be attempted if we are to retain quality. Carefully selecting the pieces of work that you are going to mark in such a way that they inform learning is the way to make marking successful. That being said, if you mark an individual pupil's work and notice a cause for concern then you should skip back through their book and mark linked work so as to get a clear picture of the learning needs of that particular pupil, focusing particularly on how any misconceptions may have developed.

So what should marking look like? This is something that schools worry about (mainly for inspection purposes I might add). Let us be blunt – marking is for you (to inform your planning) and for pupils (to inform their next steps and identify areas for development). If the marking policy isn't supporting both of these points then it is ineffective. Marking is an excellent way to differentiate. One of the tools I use is 'active marking'. This is where the process becomes a learning dialogue between teacher and pupil and is personalised to learning needs, highlighted when the pupil's work is assessed. It is a process that requires time and thought and so is not something that can be applied to every piece of work (I advise marking a piece of work every week or every two weeks) to monitor progress. Essentially it involves placing a post-it note in a pupil's book that challenges learning based upon evidence in the pupil's work. A green post-it note will mean that learning is secure and on it is a question that challenges learning further. A blue post-it note means that there are some areas that need to be further developed and the feedback and the question will illustrate this. A pink post-it note means that learning is not secure and there are key concerns and feedback will reinforce basic concepts. The purpose is that pupils then respond to these questions and they are later collected and stuck onto their learning profile sheet (this contains all post-it notes to date and gives a very clear indication of areas of weakness and strength – something easy to access for every pupil and for you, at any point, to see real-time assessment information for all key topics – very useful for revision purposes and personalising learning). You might allocate 'bell work' to pupils completing their question or you might expect them to do this for home learning. Either way, the important part of this process is that, unlike a comment written in their books that they most likely never read (and often these are generic phrases written by teachers trying to think of something to write and a target for the pupil – again to satisfy a marking policy), they have to read and synthesise the comment on the post-it note in order to answer the question. This then informs the teacher and the pupil of areas of development and learning can be differentiated accordingly. For example, if you cover a specific topic and the majority of pupils are blue (post-it) or pink (post-it) then it suggests that you need to re-visit this topic from a different angle or, if you complete a topic and all pupils are green, then you might want to expand this further to extend learning. It also provides much more detailed information than a mark in a book. Why? Because you and your pupils can clearly see specific areas within a topic. A score in a mark-book will give you just that – a numerical score. It tells you nothing more than, for example, 'in expanding brackets they scored eight out of ten'. What we are interested in is what that individual pupil did well and what they need to develop further – one pupil scoring eight out of ten could do so for different reasons and have different areas for development. Taking this one step further, those teachers who use red, amber and green in their mark-books to indicate a weak, average or strong performance in a particular area know only that – they do not know what specifically made one pupil red when compared with another, or one pupil green when compared with another. Using active marking allows you to identify, at any point in time, specific areas of strength and weakness within an area of work.

A further issue to raise in this section is the use of grades. Grading work is controversial and grades can have a negative impact on learning (sometimes they are quite demotivating). In addition the grading system is intended to provide an overview of performance and is not necessarily allocated to a particular topic. For example, if a pupil is working on a topic that is 'grade A' and they don't achieve the learning objectives does that make them a grade B? Common sense indicates that this is not really appropriate and the very best way to indicate performance (which is what we are basically doing when we grade work) is to use an indication of whether pupils are on target, above target or below target (T, T+ or T-). This then tracks progress. Be aware also that research suggests that pupils do not benefit from grades and marks on their work (Black *et al.*, 2003) and that when grades and comments are given the positive effects of the comment are detracted by the grade. Several research studies have been conducted to examine the impact of grades and comment-based marking. A study by Ruth Butler (Butler, 1988) indicated that if staff provided diagnostic comments and a grade then they may as well have just written the grade and saved time; the impact on the cohort of pupils given both the grade and comment was the same as those given just the grade. However, those provided with comment-only marking performed, on average, 30 per cent higher in the next lesson than they did in the first lesson. Of the pupils given grades, those with a low grade didn't want to continue the work and those with a high grade did. Take a moment to reflect – this probably aptly summarises what we see on a daily basis (the disheartening effect of a low grade and the motivating effect of a high grade, and the way in which pupils immediately relate this to 'how good they are at something' and can switch off or decide that they simply 'don't like the subject'). The research leads us to the conclusion that, if we are to inform learning and make feedback a powerful part of this process, then we should use comment-only marking and this is why active marking is a useful tool.

Another aspect of marking is self- and peer-assessment. This also creates choices for pupils. How well they have done informs their next steps. It is important that this is a meaningful activity and that pupils benefit from the process. This is why we need to develop their skills in assessing their own and other's work. This can be done in a variety of ways but it is best started early and certainly at the beginning of the year as a reminder – perhaps as an activity where pupils (in pairs or in a small group works well) assess a piece of work that you have prepared (Bartlett, 2015). Peer-assessment is the best way to start and then progress to self-assessment. It has to be more than an exercise in ticking and crossing (which is often how pupils perceive 'marking' work) – it is a process of assessing work. Pupils need to develop their metacognition, becoming more autonomous, identifying their learning needs and shaping the direction of their own learning. Start by giving pupils examples of good, average and poor feedback, ask them to identify each and then identify the key features of what makes feedback 'good' and what makes it 'bad'. Then, as a class, develop a set of guidelines and use these as a framework when pupils assess learning. The key feature of peer- and self-assessment when related to differentiation is the questions that it generates. These questions are generated by the pupils themselves and time must be given to allowing them to address these questions. If we simply assess learning and move on then this places little value on the activity and the powerful effect it has on learning is diminished. It is an opportunity for a 'think, pair, share' exercise where pupils engage in discussion with others to develop their own learning or to support others (remember teaching someone is an excellent way to embed learning). Therefore, use assessment as learning in a formative way to develop and identify next steps. This supports a differentiated pathway in learning.

Climate for learning

The climate for learning is extremely important for differentiation to work well. We require a safe environment for pupils to be able to assess their work and to support one another to make progress. It is important they feel included. We want to encourage open debate and discussion about learning – where pupils question themselves and others. If pupils feel concerned about getting something wrong or about others perhaps ridiculing an answer then they will not share their thoughts (human nature). It is therefore very important to think about the climate you want to create. You need to have rules and expectations for behaviour and you need to develop a culture where pupils 'have a go' and are willing to highlight any misconceptions they have.

For pupils to succeed they need to believe they can learn (self-belief) and that what they are learning is useful, relevant and meaningful to them (teachers' planning). As a teacher we also have to impose our belief that pupils can achieve and be successful. The brain is a complex organ. It is a parallel processor facilitating learning by involving both focused attention and peripheral perception. The peripheral perception is related to the learning environment – external stimuli (posters in the room, displays of pupil work, colour of the walls, subtle looks or gestures that convey meaning are all interpreted by the brain). If pupils experience stress then the emotional centres of the brain take control of cognitive function and thinking is not as efficient. Consequently learning or learning potential is affected (negatively). It is important to challenge learning and to remember that when teachers teach to the middle the more able will potentially disengage (it becomes boring and too easy) but the less able will be placed under emotional stress (impeding their learning). Differentiation is therefore essential to engage all learners and allow all learners the opportunity to succeed. Taking this further, once the levels of readiness have been considered then pupils can be grouped accordingly, accommodating different levels of understanding. Classrooms that promote pupil choice and embed routines that demonstrate mutual respect are supportive learning environments for all pupils and differentiation underpins this.

It is important to think about your body language as well as your verbal response. Pupils easily pick up on 'us'. For example, a low-ability pupil surprises you with their explanation – if you allow that surprise to show (raised eyebrows, wide eyes) then the pupil will immediately pick up on that and it shows the pupil that you weren't expecting that answer from them. This can have a negative impact and limit their potential – they revert to 'what you expect of them'. At the opposite end of the spectrum, if a more-able pupil is not able to answer a question or gives a poor response then a disappointed look can lead them to being less comfortable in answering in the future. They lose confidence (they haven't lived up to the expectation – yours and their own – of them being able to answer correctly). Therefore, be very conscious of your body language. Also, when responding verbally to a question, think about the language you use. Again if you actually say 'well done. I wasn't expecting that from you' then a pupil feels as if you are categorising them as a lower-ability pupil. Reinforcing this thought can limit their likelihood of 'having a go' because they feel you have low expectations of them and they start to have low expectations of themselves. It is also important for all pupils to experience 'failure' (take this as it is meant) and to then have to unpick something to get to the correct answer. This prevents the emotional downturn if a more-able pupil doesn't get everything right (it is less 'catastrophic' for them). They begin to understand that we all sometimes get things wrong; it's how we then unpick a misconception and work towards a solution that is the essential skill that all pupils need to learn.

Our physical surroundings are also very important. Think how you feel if you go into a 'nice' classroom – one with clear displays of pupils' work and a clean and ordered working environment. Now consider how you feel when you walk into a classroom with dirty desks, graffiti on tables, posters or displays ripped and an untidy working environment. Pupils are sensitive to these physical stimuli. To create a positive learning environment we should rotate our displays and use pupils' work. This doesn't have to be work specifically completed for display purposes but photos of work in progress. What is important is that it is updated and kept 'fresh'. Another idea is to use interactive displays that form part of the learning environment (Bartlett, 2015). When we involve displays in our teaching they become more than simply a poster on a wall that pupils rarely look at (or rather rarely use to develop their learning). Active displays form part of the learning process and can be as simple as using the displays in some way to find out information.

Summary

Assessment for learning and differentiation work in tandem. The evidence from assessment informs future learning pathways and our differentiated pathways ensure that assessment best supports learning. Both summative and formative assessment are used to determine where we pitch learning. Summative assessment is typically used to give us a global overview of pupil performance (results of a test which covers a unit of work or periodic assessment). Formative assessment is crucial to informing differentiated pathways during the lesson as learning is taking place. When we use formative assessment in the classroom it is important that we operate in a safe learning environment where pupils are comfortable making mistakes and learning from them and at the same time in judging their own and their peer's performance and receiving constructive feedback. When we plan for learning we need to consider:

- Does prior data inform planning?
- How do we use data?
- Is learning pitched at the right level?
- How is learning assessed?
- Does formative assessment direct learning pathways during the learning process?
- Do the outcomes of the assessments support pupils' next steps?
- Do the outcomes of the assessments support pupil choice?
- Is assessment data accurate and reliable?
- Is the learning environment safe with a positive climate for learning?
- Do we celebrate success and challenge misconceptions?
- Do we have high expectations of all pupils?
- Does assessment drive progress and ensure learning is accessible to all?
- Do marking and feedback inform progress?

CHAPTER 7

Questioning and differentiation

Questioning is one of the most powerful techniques available to us, commonly used to develop, challenge and assess learning. Complex theories on cognitive development underpin the techniques we use. During teacher training or ongoing professional development you will no doubt have been exposed to research that has been translated for our practice in the classroom. How often, though, do you use this to enhance learning in your classroom? Are you conscious of the different techniques when you apply questioning? How often do you evaluate your own practice? Not only must we develop our questioning techniques, but also encourage pupils to develop the questions that they ask – creating the enquiring mind.

Take a moment to reflect:

- How many questions do you think that you ask a day?
- What percentage do you think are procedural (classroom management)?
- What percentage do you think require simply recall of fact or knowledge?
- What percentage develop higher-order thinking skills and really challenge thinking?
- Do you think that you effectively develop learning through questioning?
- Do you differentiate through questioning?
- How long do you wait before you expect an answer?
- How long do you wait before you respond to an answer?
- Do all pupils in your classroom leave having answered at least one question?
- How do you facilitate questioning?
- Who asks the questions?
- Are pupils asking questions of you, themselves and each other that demonstrate higher-order skills?

There are numerous academic studies that focus on questioning and research suggests that teachers ask between 300 and 400 questions a day (Levin and Long, 1981). The first thing we should be asking ourselves is 'what is the quality of these questions?' The results of many studies suggest that of these questions 'approximately 60% of questions are lower order, 20% are higher order and 20% are procedural' (Cotton, 1988). More worryingly, Kerry (1998) reports that, in observing a number of lessons, he found that at least 60 per cent of questions asked were recall questions, with 12–30 per cent more being management questions (for example, 'would you sit down please?'), leaving only approximately 4 per cent of questions being of a higher order or open in nature. Both researchers indicate that the majority of our questions focus on recall or knowledge-based facts and that a much smaller percentage of our questions develop higher-order thinking skills. The spectrum is therefore weighted to low-level cognitive skills, suggesting that we assess the majority of pupils (through questioning) on their ability to recall rather than their ability to think deeply and we therefore limit our challenge of learning. The other question we must ask ourselves is that if we are asking less than 20 per cent higher-order questions then who are we targeting? Is it the same pupils? This of course would apply a glass ceiling to those who never experience the more thought-provoking questions and, sadly (but typically), teachers ask those pupils who they think will be able to answer the question correctly. This is particularly the case in an observed lesson where there is the perception that pupils giving a correct answer must therefore understand and this indicates that the rest of the class have grasped the concept, thus almost using questioning in a reassuring way for the teacher as, if the pupil they ask gets it right, then the teacher infers that they must be teaching it correctly. Consequently, the less able tend to be asked low-level questions and the more able higher-level questions. This of course limits learning and is a poor example of differentiation through questioning. This chapter challenges this approach.

Questioning is one of the most powerful pedagogical techniques, yet one that is underestimated and often underused. Why is this, given that this forms a significant part of our daily dialogue? Research based on teachers' use of questioning in the classroom suggests that 'questioning was not an easy mediating artefact to develop partly because many teachers felt that they were already doing it and often failed to appreciate its full potential for enabling dialogue that could develop thinking' (Webb and Jones, 2009). This may be because teachers feel that since they already use questioning in their lessons they must be doing it well. In reality it is hard to change something that is already so heavily embedded in a teacher's daily practice and we need to employ clear strategies for development. Many teachers also think that questioning does not require careful planning (and this is because it is something that is so frequently and naturally used – both in our teaching and daily lives – it is a skill). Of course, as you develop your questioning ability, then this may more likely be the case. However, in order to ensure we ask higher-order questions, we need to think carefully about the questions in advance (otherwise in reality what happens is that teachers default to lower-level questions). Questioning needs to be developed and it may be appropriate to begin with lower-order questions, progressing to higher-order questions. It is important to plan some questions in advance of the lesson in order to stimulate discussion. Key questions should be developed that will help students to deepen their understanding and that will act as critical starting points for further debate. In this chapter we look at how we do this while, at the same time, ensuring that all pupils are exposed to higher order questions and that we differentiate and target questioning to support progress for all pupils. 'Who questions much, shall learn much and retain much' (Francis Bacon).

So, why do we use questioning in the classroom? Listed below are a few ideas:

- to determine knowledge;
- to gauge understanding;
- to encourage motivation;
- to stimulate thinking;
- to show an interest;
- to develop a problem;
- to clarify ideas;
- to challenge;
- to support behaviour management.

These are but a few of the reasons teachers use questioning in the classroom and I leave you to think about whether any one or more of the above dominate in your lesson. Think carefully about the importance of questioning in your classroom – how you use questioning and the reasons why you use questioning. Next time you are teaching, consciously process your use of questioning.

Wait time and hands down

There are two different aspects of 'wait time':

- the time you wait before asking a pupil to respond (thinking time);
- the time you wait before responding to their answer (response time).

Both of these are extremely important when using questioning to develop learning in the classroom. Next time you are teaching make a note of the time you typically allocate to each of the above (I would imagine that, on average, it is very short). Common sense tells us that if we are asking a question that requires pupils to really think (typically a higher-order question) then we need to allow sufficient time for pupils to process the question and to synthesise their response. But how long do you wait? It may or may not surprise you to know that research suggests that the average wait time for the response to a question is one second or less (Cotton, 1988). Let's put this into context, if I asked you a challenging question and then expected an answer in less than a second then you are likely to stumble (we create pressure – emotional stress). For quick-fire questions that are lower order we would typically expect to see a shorter response time. For example, if I asked pupils '3 × 4', I would expect them to very quickly (and probably within a second) return an answer of 12. This type of question is simply a test of recall or memory. However, if I ask a pupil to explain to me which is the longest side of a right-angle triangle and why, I would need to allow a longer response time – it is the 'why' that creates this situation (recall would simply be telling me that it is the hypotenuse but the 'why' involves them explaining). Short thinking time coupled with rapid teacher response tells us immediately that there is little opportunity beyond low-level cognitive development and the quality of answers is poor (when compared with extended processing time). Therefore, the impact of questioning to support learning is of variable quality. If you extend pupils' thinking time to three seconds or more for lower-order cognitive questions, and to more than seven seconds for higher-order cognitive questions, you will see that the quality of discussion/response improves. Research suggests a strong positive correlation between student outcomes and wait time (Cotton, 1988). It may initially feel uncomfortable having a silent pause – because if you count to seven you will see that this does feel quite long – but it allows pupils time to think (although be sure not to identify who will answer the question until the thinking time is up so that all pupils remain involved). Therefore, if we are to maximise the impact of questioning on learning, there is much more to think about than simply the question itself.

Now we address an old favourite: 'no hands up'. This is a simple yet incredibly valuable technique to use in your classroom. 'No hands up' means exactly that – you ask a question to the whole class, allow thinking (processing) time and only then identify the pupil who is to respond first. This is, of course, differentiation in practice because we are exposing all pupils to the question but targeting the response. This may sound obvious but be honest – do you always adopt a hands-down policy? If you do then that is fantastic and if you don't then it's time to change. Unfortunately, a lot of teachers ask a question and, even if they allow thinking time, they wait for hands to shoot up and then pick a pupil to answer. Of course some teachers may do this and then pick someone with their hand down (but this is not common). When teachers adopt this practice you will find that if you map the room and place a cross by pupils who answer a question then, usually, by the end of the lesson, there are clusters of crosses in the same areas and this indicates that the same pupils answer the majority of questions. What we would want to see is an even distribution of crosses across the classroom. Taking this one step further, if we map the level of the question (lower order to higher order) then you often see the same pupils answering lower-order questions and the same pupils answering higher-order questions. Again, if we are to differentiate learning correctly and ensure all pupils make progress, then we want to see an even distribution across the lesson or series of lessons. So why do teachers invite hands up? In all honesty it is most likely to be because (as discussed above) when a pupil answers correctly we feel (subconsciously) as though we must be doing our job (they clearly understand what we have taught and we take the single pupil as indicative of the class). Seeking the correct answer in this fashion is known as evaluative listening (Davies, 1997). In reality, all that teachers achieve from evaluative listening is to find out whether pupils know what they want them to know or know what they have taught, and it is often seen when teachers feel a necessity to stick to their 'lesson plan'. Some teachers also feel that when pupils put their hands up to respond it provides an indication of engagement with learning – if 30 pupils are keen to respond then you know that you are engaging minds but if it is only one or two then, perhaps, it is not pitched at the right level. The reality of 'hands-up' is that we are giving pupils the option of whether to participate or not. In other words, pupils can actively choose to disengage. If we take that choice away by expecting all pupils to synthesise the question and create that cliff hanger where any one of them could be picked to answer, then we limit the possibility of pupils switching off – they have to pay attention because it could be them. Targeting questioning in this way allows you to differentiate and ensure that all learners are challenged and we do not limit learning.

Let us now address different questioning techniques. Two that are commonly used are the ping-pong style and the basketball style. The ping-pong style is typically used for quick-fire low-level questions that simply require recall and test basic knowledge (think of a times-tables test). Essentially, the question goes from you to the pupil and back to you for a final response (typically correct or incorrect) and you ask another direct question. Your input is high and immediately after the first response. This type of questioning is not suitable when we wish to develop learning. In this scenario it is important to use basketball-style questioning (keep your input minimal). What this means is that you ask a question, allow for thinking time, identify the first person to respond and then allow for response time. In this response time you expect all pupils to think about the answer they have just heard. You can then identify another pupil to add their thoughts or to develop the answer further, and so on. You may need to dispense a few added thoughts or comment but, essentially, you are developing the answer through the 'team' rather than only through a single pupil, and then back to you for the final response, and then a new question (a question and answer approach). A single question is therefore extended and developed much more and we embrace the opportunity to discuss misconceptions as part of this forum. Remember that wrong answers are important when assessing and developing learning because they allow us to highlight and unpick any misconceptions, encouraging pupils to think about the 'why' and the 'why not', and they allow us to identify future learning paths (we may need to redirect learning). When pupils think about why an answer is not correct they are using higher-order thinking skills and this is an essential part of cognitive development.

Open and closed questions

There are two different types of question – open questions and closed questions. They are different in character and in how we use them. An open question stimulates thinking and naturally encourages higher-order cognitive development. It will often lead to discussions encouraging pupils to think and reflect, offering opinion and feelings. For example:

- What emotions does the writer evoke?
- What makes the leaves change colour?
- Under what conditions is this equation not valid?

- Why is it important to purify water?
- What do you think the artist was thinking?
- Why is light important to plants?
- How did the poem make you feel?

Closed questions are lower order and typically require recall, knowledge or, at their simplest level, a 'yes' or 'no' response. For example:

- Is 25 a square number?
- What kind of painting is this?
- What era do you think this is from?
- Is Paris the capital of France?
- What is the capital of Spain?
- What are the elements of hydrochloric acid?
- Did the poem make you feel happy?

As discussed above, a closed question is typically associated with ping-pong questioning (typically diagnostic – factual recall) and an open question with basketball questioning (typically discussion-based). An open question creates opportunities for cognitive development and is typically extended to higher-order thinking skills. Open questions lead to valuable learning discussion and debate but are not good diagnostic questions. Diagnostic questions need no discussion because they provide concrete evidence about the pupils' learning. 'What makes a question useful as a diagnostic question, therefore, is that it must be very unlikely that the student gets the correct answer for the wrong reasons' (Wiliam, 2011). Many teachers develop questioning in their classroom by beginning with a closed question and developing this to an open question, which they bounce around the room (basketball questioning). For example, take the closed question 'is 8 a cube number?' The answer is, of course, 'yes'. If we know that pupils already have an understanding of cube numbers and this question is simply used as a test of knowledge then we may leave it there. If, however, we want to probe learning further then the most obvious next question is 'why?' Following from this we might ask pupils whether 6 is a cube number and to explain their answer. This may lead to pupils being asked to identify the cube numbers between 50 and 200. If you choose to do this then you need to be very aware of to whom you are asking the lower-order question and ensure that it is not the same pupils every lesson, and to allow time for discussion. It is important to differentiate questioning appropriately, but not so as to apply a glass ceiling to learning. Many open questions can be answered by the less-able pupil through supportive techniques such as scaffolding and we discuss this in the following section. Remember that questioning is used for many purposes but the key points are to develop learning (developing a concept) and to assess learning. The outcomes of both determine next steps and so questioning itself determines differentiated pathways for pupils as well as being a tool to differentiate.

Bloom's Taxonomy

You will no doubt have encountered Bloom's Taxonomy (Bloom and Krathwohl, 1956) during your teaching career. Bloom classifies questions according to their level of cognitive demand and the taxonomy is an excellent tool when designing questions with different purposes or learning objectives. In this section we discuss an adaptation of Bloom's Taxonomy by a group of cognitive psychologists, led by Anderson (a former student of Bloom) in the 1990s. Anderson updated the taxonomy to reflect relevance to twenty-first-century work (Anderson and Krathwohl, 2001, pp. 67-68). The new system contains six levels that are based on hierarchical form (as with Bloom) and that move from the lowest level of cognition (thinking) to the highest level of cognition: remembering, understanding, applying, analysing, evaluating, creating (this compares with Bloom's original taxonomy of: knowledge, comprehension, application, analysis, synthesis and evaluation). Note that 'the top two levels are essentially exchanged from the old to the new version' (Schultz, 2005) and that there is a movement from nouns to verbs such as, for example, 'application' to 'applying'.

In the remainder of this section we look at the different classifications of questions and how to use these to develop learning. The important point to remember is that lower-order questions are not for low-ability pupils. All pupils of all ages and abilities need to be exposed to the higher-order questions and it is how we do this that underpins our differentiation strategy. Each type of question has its own importance and value in learning – what we have to be is very clear on the purpose of each question we ask and what it tells us about learning in the classroom.

Remembering

Remembering is the lowest level and simply involves the recall of facts. For example:

1) What is 5×7?
2) What is the formula for the circumference of a circle?
3) What is the formula for the volume of a sphere?
4) What are the elements of sulphuric acid?
5) Which letters are vowels?
6) What is the capital of Australia?
7) List the rules for netball.
8) What is the name for a multi-channelled river?
9) *Qu'est-ce que c'est?* (flashcards).
10) Who painted the Mona-Lisa?
11) Can you identify the boundary lines in the gym?

Generic prompts include: What did…? Who did…? How many…?
   Words often used: know, who, define, what, name, where, list, when.

Understanding

Understanding facts and ideas by organising, classifying, comparing, translating, inter-preting, giving descriptions and stating the main ideas from oral, written or graphic representations. For example:

1) What is the main idea of this story?
2) How do waves erode the coast?
3) Can you write a brief outline?
4) Why are both −5 and 5 the square root of 25?
5) Describe the climate graph.
6) What does the ratio 5:2 mean?
7) How would you illustrate the water cycle?
8) Who was the key character?
9) Can you explain how to convert your 6–second heart rate count into beats per minute?
10) *Ecoute la cassette et remplis la grille.*
11) What is the subject or theme of the picture (art)?
12) Explain what strategies you used to get your teammates free in this game.

Generic prompts include: Why did…? What are/does…? Why has…? Can you explain…?

Words often used include: describe, use your own words to, outline, explain, discuss, compare.

Applying

Applying is where pupils take information they already know and apply it to different situations to reach a solution. Examples include:

1) How would you use your knowledge of longitude and latitude to locate Greenland?
2) If there were 8 inches of water in this tank and all you have is a hose, how would you empty all of the water out?
3) Do you know another instance where…?
4) What factors would change if…?
5) What questions would you ask of…?
6) Why does the climate graph show this pattern?
7) How would you change the activity to reach the target heart rate?
8) A supermarket is offering 3 for 2 on its products. A small bag of 80 teabags cost £1.40 and a large bag of 320 teabags cost £3.70. Milo wants to buy 320 teabags. Which is the better deal?
9) How do you round a number to the nearest 100?
10) How would you describe the stages the artist may have gone through from start to finish to complete this painting?
11) How might your painting be different?

12) How would you compare and contrast the two sports of lacrosse and football before we begin our next unit?

13) Given what you have just learned, how could you devise a better way of doing the experiment?

Generic prompts: How can you…? How would you…? Using this information can you…?

Words often used include: apply, demonstrate, calculate, illustrate, classify, discover, solve, compare.

Analysing

Analysing involves pupils breaking down a problem and looking at it in different ways. Pupils need to provide reasons and reach conclusions using evidence to support their argument, and they need to have a strong awareness of how component parts relate to one another. Examples include:

1) Why do we call these animals mammals?
2) If…happened what would the outcome have been?
3) Why did…changes occur?
4) Can you explain what must have happened when…?
5) Give pupils two different graphs that offer similar information such as, for example, boys' and girls' heights in a box plot. Ask pupils to analyse the information and come to conclusions.
6) Analyse the strategies used in the first and second round of the game.
7) Explain why, if we increase 80 by 25 per cent, we add the same amount as we take off if we decrease the answer by 20 per cent.
8) What are some of the factors that cause rust?
9) Why did the UK declare war with Germany on 4th August 1914?
10) What was the turning point in the game?
11) What elements of art (line, shape, space, form, texture, colour) did the artist use?
12) What is the function of regeneration projects?
13) What is the artist's main message in their painting?
14) Why is the website for business A more successful than the website for business B?

Generic prompts: What are…? Why did…? Why do…? What if…? Consider…? Discuss….

Words used include: analyse, connect, arrange, compare, select, explain, infer, order.

Evaluating

Evaluating is where pupils make connections, engage in creative thinking and justify decisions through checking and critiquing. They present and defend opinions, making judgements about the validity of information or quality of work based on key criteria. These questions naturally illicit different responses. Examples include:

1) Which poem did you feel best represented the feeling of loss?
2) Which character do you like the best?
3) Imagine you could climb inside the painting. How do you feel?
4) Why do you think (insert name) is so famous?
5) Judge the value of....
6) What changes to…would you recommend?
7) Is there a better solution to…?
8) List two fractions that lie between ⅓ and ½.
9) Which management choice is likely to have the most positive impact?
10) Which was the better strategy to use?
11) *Tu préfères le système scolaire en France ou en Grande-Bretagne? Pourquoi?*
12) Why is '*Nous sommes allés à Cardiff au pays de Galles avec mon oncle et sa petite amie*' a better response to my question than '*Je suis allé en France*'?
13) Discuss whether the picture directs eye movement to the main subject of the painting.
14) Construct an argument to support your decision to choose that game strategy over another.
15) How well does this music create a sense of suspense?

Generic prompts: How would you…? Construct a…? Are everybody's results the same…?

Words used include: prepare, generalise, create, plan, substitute, modify.

Creating

Creating is where pupils create a new or alternative solution by combining information or elements in a different way. To accomplish 'creating' tasks, learners generate, plan and produce. Examples include:

1) How would you assemble these items to create a windmill?
2) How would you complete the circuit?
3) Create two different sequences where the fourth term is 12 and write down the general rule for both of them.
4) The answer contains Cl_2 what was the question?
5) Put these words together to create a complete sentence.
6) Can you see a possible solution to....
7) Can you design a new recipe for a dish that contains …?
8) How would your life be different if you could breathe underwater? How would we need to be adapted?
9) In what ways would you render the subject differently(art)?

10) Design a pocket guide to fair testing.
11) Compose a piece of music to convey one of these emotions….

Generic prompts: What would have happened if…? Pretend that….Design a….Think of another way to….

Words used include: assess, design, create, develop.

Now we have discussed the taxonomy of questions it is important to look at how we use differentiation to ensure that all pupils have access to higher-order questions. Far too often teachers resort to asking low-ability pupils low-level questions and their learning is therefore not challenged and their development limited. They never have the opportunity to think more deeply. Let us take a higher-order question and think carefully about how we might develop the question to ensure that all learners can access it (of course these questions can be verbal or written).

'What led to the flooding at Waterlogged?'

This is a very open question ('Waterlogged' is a fictitious place), one that requires deep thought and one that possibly only a few of the more-able learners will be able to access or contribute to as a direct open question. If, however, we scaffold the question by asking a series of questions that develop learning and support pupils in formulating an argument (effectively encouraging thinking through questioning) then we may use something like this:

* 'Can you describe the landscape surrounding Waterlogged?'
* 'How was the weather linked to the flooding?'
* 'What happened to the water once it had hit the ground?'

Questioning can continue in this way to generate ideas – you can then ask any pupil to develop this further based upon the whole-class discussion. It supports access, guides learning and gives all pupils the opportunity (albeit in a more structured manner) to think about the initial question (what led to the flooding at Waterlogged?). If you look carefully at the three questions they move from knowledge (can you describe…) to analysis (what happened to…).

Now it's your turn. One of the things I encourage all teachers to do is to observe a colleague's lesson and to get someone to observe your lesson or video your lesson (within school policy). Make the questioning the focus of the observation. Use the technique I discussed at the start of this chapter. Make a plan of the room and map who you ask questions to and the level of those questions. Also focus on your 'hands down' policy, wait time and response time (this is easier when a lesson is videoed as you can reflect on practice). Take time to plan a few key questions for your next lesson and think about their level in terms of Bloom's Taxonomy. Take a higher-order question and think carefully about how you might scaffold it to ensure a less-able pupil can access the learning. Use the techniques we have discussed in this chapter to deepen your awareness of questioning to support all learners. If you have a conscious awareness of questioning in the classroom then your use of questioning to develop learning will improve.

Goldilocks and the Three Bears

We all know the story of *Goldilocks and the Three Bears* (Ladybird, 2008). This is often used in schools as training material to develop questioning techniques. I use it here so that you can see how we can ask different levels of questions, each of which require increased cognitive ability.

Knowledge: Who was the biggest bear? What food was too hot?

Comprehension: Why didn't the bears eat the porridge? Why did the bears leave their house?

Application: List the sequence of events in the story. Draw three pictures showing the beginning, middle and end of the story.

Analysis: Why do you think Goldilocks went to have a sleep? What kind of person do you think Goldilocks is and why?

Synthesis: How could you re-write the story in a city setting? Write a set of rules to prevent what happened in the story.

Evaluation: Why has this story stood the test of time? If this happened in the modern day and Goldilocks was arrested, make a case for the prosecution and for the defence. Write a review of this story for a newspaper.

If you want all pupils to complete the evaluative activity based on the court room then the more able may be able to do this with no support but the less able may need the question to be scaffolded. The way to do this is to think of the end scenario (the courtroom outcome) and then formulate a series of questions that will help the learner develop. For instance you may ask 'did Goldilocks have a right to enter the house?', 'did Goldilocks cause any damage in the house?' and so on. This leads learning in the desired direction and enables all pupils to access the higher-order question (we are taking a differentiated approach to questioning).

'Think, pair, share'

Another way in which we develop a question in the classroom is to use strategies such as 'think, pair, share'. This is a cognitive rehearsal strategy that, as the name suggests, encourages pupils to think about a question individually for a minute or so, then to form a discussion pair where they share their ideas and ask questions of each other, and then a sharing of ideas in a larger group or whole class forum where pupils discuss and question ideas (it is also referred to as 'snowballing' when the pair form a four and the four then form an eight, and so on, until the whole class becomes the final group).

The point we will focus on in this section is the questions that pupils ask each other. This is a skill that is important to develop. Pupils need to ask the right questions in order to get the answers they need and we know this is highly skilled. Socratic questioning is one technique. Socratic questioning underpins the philosophy that thinking is driven by questions. In terms of the 'think, pair, share' exercise we would expect the individual thought to promote questions in the paired discussion that will generate further thinking and then, in turn, more questions. Developing pupils' questioning skills is important. Think about the average primary school classroom – pupils ask lots of questions. So what happens when we get to secondary school? The amount of questions pupils ask seems to rapidly diminish – pupils seem to become conditioned to being 'told' something, accept it as fact and don't question it; we need to reverse this and promote a culture of asking 'why'.

Developing a concept through questioning

The technique discussed in this section is very powerful for engaging pupils early in the thinking process. Essentially we encourage pupils to think for themselves and to develop key concepts through a series of cleverly-engineered questions. The general rule of thumb is that, if you are going to tell a pupil how to do something or what to do, then think about whether you can turn this into a question that will encourage the pupil to think for themselves. This develops much better learners than those who are forced to memorise hundreds of facts through knowledge-based teaching. It also creates pupils who can make connections in their learning.

To keep this simple we look here at metaphors (something we will all be familiar with). This will allow us to focus more on the technique than the specific subject content. Metaphors are often introduced to the class in a taught fashion – pupils are told what a metaphor is and then they complete an activity based on the definition they have been told. Turning this around, we can involve pupils in their own learning and increase their thinking by giving them a set of sentences containing metaphors and then asking them to decide what are the common factors (unpicking in this way requires deeper thought). These can be differentiated by task – giving different metaphors to pupils of different ability. Once pupils have thought about the use of language we can open discussion as a whole class, leading to the definition of a metaphor. A nice activity to follow involves pupils working in groups. One group could be allocated 'colour', 'the body' or 'the weather' and so on. Each group has to think about metaphors associated with each. For example, 'to see red', 'a white lie' or 'the heart of the city', 'the foot of the mountain'. This can be a 'beat the clock' activity and we will see different outcomes. In involving pupils in the process in this way they are much more likely to remember the definition of a metaphor and to be able to provide examples using them in their creative writing.

Let us use indices as an example from mathematics (focus on the fact this is usually a rule pupils are taught and then apply rather than on the specific topic of indices). Pupils are often told the rules of indices and are then expected to memorise them parrot fashion and answer questions. This does little to enhance their comprehension. Instead, it is better to encourage pupils to develop their own understanding by experiencing indices in action. For example, you might ask pupils to expand simple expressions as a starter such as:

1) 5^4
2) 2^5
3) 7^3
4) x^4

This might lead to you asking pupils to expand a simple expression such as $2^5 \times 2^3$. In doing so they produce $2\times2\times2\times2\times2 \times 2\times2\times2$, which they can simplify to 2^8. Further attempts at similar questions will lead them to the general rule that when we multiply terms of the same base then we add the indices. The same process can be repeated for division and negative indices. Understanding can be checked through a few quick-fire questions, such as:

1) $4^3 \times 4^7$
2) $5^2 \times 5^{43}$
3) $60^3 \times 60^{22}$

Questioning can be used to check that the underlying concepts are secure and questions that focus on errors can be used to check understanding. Pupils might be asked to correct the following statements (common errors):

1) $5^2 \times 5^3 = 25^5$
2) $3^4 \times 2^7 = 6^{11}$

In asking pupils to explain you are requiring them to use higher-order thinking skills and the power is in the 'why'. This may then lead to class discussion of more challenging questions. The results of a subsequent mini-assessment will guide differentiated pathways – typically differentiation by task with a tiered worksheet where the more able may combine knowledge with other skills and application. The emphasis, again, is on involving pupils in developing concepts rather than telling them and expecting them to store knowledge-based information for later recall. Developing learning through thinking is an extremely powerful technique.

Teacher input

As a teacher you do not want to intervene too early when you have asked a question. Getting the balance of teacher input right can take a lot of practice and, of course, it also depends on your audience. However, there are key points when a teacher or facilitator does need to intervene:

- When pupils need subject-specific notation or words.
- During consolidation to offer alternative methods or to highlight key features.

- When pupils need guidance. This can be where the lesson is pulled back follow-ing on-going assessment.

It is also important, once we have asked a question, for us to intervene in a positive way by digging deeper. Questions such as: 'Why do you think that?', 'Would your answer change if I told you…?', 'Can you think of a piece of evidence to back that up…?', 'Can you justify what you have said…?', 'How do you think that relates to the question?' act by attempting to really explore how pupils arrived at their origi-nal answer – essentially asking for justification and explanation. This differentiates because it helps pupils to think about the understanding that underpins their thinking and pupils can explore these sorts of questions at their own level.

When and how a teacher intervenes still remains a controversial topic. Some research suggests that, in those countries where teachers 'talk' more during lessons, pupils actually perform better than in countries where they talk less (Wiliam, 2011). I argue that it is the quality of the teacher input that is the key factor in pupil per-formance. Of course with any studies that involve live subjects it is difficult to make such generalisations as so many variables come into play, so we must consider this when reviewing research.

Summary

Questioning is an essential feature of any lesson and it is the quality of our question-ing that leads to outstanding learning. Research tells us that the majority of questions asked in a lesson are lower order and that we need to make a conscious effort to plan key questions (higher order) prior to the lesson. Other questions will branch naturally off these using the techniques that we have discussed in this chapter. Ques-tioning should be used to draw out learning and probe understanding, and we can differentiate questioning by the type of questions we ask (be careful not to target low-level questions at low-ability learners) and by how we ask them (scaffolding ques-tions where appropriate). The outcomes of questioning sessions are used to assess learning and inform future pathways or redirect as necessary.

When you plan your next lesson:

- Establish clear learning outcomes.
- Ensure that you have thought about three key questions to develop during the lesson that link to each outcome (there may only be one learning outcome but several success criteria).
- Think about how you might scaffold these questions to support pupils in achiev-ing the desired outcomes.
- Think about possible questions that might branch from these key questions.
- Be aware of possible misconceptions that may arise.
- Be aware of the purpose of questioning – what does answering that question achieve and how does it support pupil progress?

- Develop the vocabulary associated with higher-order thinking.
- Develop concepts through questioning – avoid telling pupils a series of facts or how to do something (knowledge-based teaching).
- Don't just use 'whole class questioning' – develop questioning through 'think, pair, share' or other group activities.
- Be aware of 'to whom' you are asking which type of question and ensure that all pupils are exposed to higher-order questions – have high expectations of all pupils.
- Promote a safe learning environment where mistakes are valued as part of the learning process and where pupils are confident to answer questions and to ask questions of you, themselves and their peers.

'It is not that I'm so smart. But I stay with the questions much longer.'

Albert Einstein

CHAPTER 8

Embedding differentiation

Differentiation is not an isolated practice and often, when we have so many different whole school policies for one thing or another, we suggest that one policy operates independently from another. Of course this is not the case. Our teaching and learning strategies need to be applied with common sense and as a combination of techniques – they are not mutually exclusive. Take assessment for learning and differentiation for example. Without assessing learning we cannot differentiate. Why? Simply because how do we know where to start, the pathway each pupil should take and then how do we know they have got there? We differentiate through questioning, for example, and yet questioning is ineffective unless we tailor it to the individual. All of our strategies are connected, and we move to a complex learning model when we consider all of the factors that contribute to an outstanding learning environment.

I ask now that you find your whole school policy for differentiation. When was the last time you looked at it (most likely the INSET session where it was handed to you)? How have you used it to inform your planning? Is it current and linked to other teaching and learning policies within the school? Who was involved in its design – was it written *for* staff or were staff involved in shaping it to tailor it to the real needs of the school? Is it something that supports you and supports pupils in the classroom? When was it last reviewed and by whom? There are lots of questions teaching staff and school leaders must ask about all policies. When a policy is imposed in a top-down fashion it is usually simply filed and rarely referred to. When we involve all staff in developing and reviewing the policy they take ownership and it means something to them – it is current and relevant to the daily practice in their classrooms in their school. Stakeholder opinion is important (but only if you absorb feedback and use it to improve). One of the things it is essential to do with all policies is to measure the impact. Are teachers applying the policy? How does it improve the quality of teaching and learning? Is the classroom experience enhanced as a result of the policy? Is pupil progress improving as a result? A follow on to each of these questions is 'how do you know?' If the policy is not understood and easily implemented by teaching staff then it will have limited impact on pupil progress. It will be nothing more than the 'new initiative', which is filed in a draw at the earliest convenience, ready to be pulled out when OFSTED visit (for example.). Policies are working documents – a rigid and static policy does little to shape the future of learning. We must invest in and support teachers (many of whom may not have experienced recent training in new pedagogies) in becoming better practitioners and, most importantly, we must quality assure that training; is the training excellent because without excellence in training how can teachers become truly outstanding practitioners? High quality training lies at the heart of improving our profession.

Just like many other pedagogies, differentiation is integral to outstanding teaching and learning. It really isn't an 'add on' but an implicit technique – something that outstanding practitioners make seem so simple and seamless. Many schools approach differentiation through an SEN policy. This is not good practice. Differentiation is for all pupils. The SEN policy must include strategies for differentiation (and the individual pupil plans will personalise this) or contribute to the differentiation policy document as a whole. When shaping your differentiation policy it is, therefore, very important to think carefully about what differentiation actually is. Once you are clear on this it is important to think about where you want to be as a school. What do you want pupils to experience in the classroom? What do you want to see when you observe a lesson? What do you want to be embedded in daily teaching practices? What is the role of each stakeholder? When you have a vision for differentiation then you can begin to think about the steps to get there. If you don't tailor your policy in this way and you simply adapt a policy perhaps from another school then, potentially, it may not work for your school. For everything you 'write' think carefully about the potential outcomes – if these don't benefit stakeholders and if it doesn't enhance learning then there is little point. Therefore, equally important as personalising learning (high on schools' agendas) is personalising policies – making sure they are right for your school. What you don't want to do is write a policy simply because it satisfies the latest government trend. Your policies should reflect your learning environment and serve to enhance the learning experience of pupils. Involve stakeholders in the process and make the document a workable policy. Remember, though, that simply having a policy is only the first step (and the easy part); the challenge is implementing it.

Introducing new techniques

Whole school teaching and learning training is usually delivered on a school INSET day. I want you to think back to the last INSET training day you attended. How useful was it (can you remember it)? Were you engaged in the training sessions (or did you simply go through the motions)? Have you used that training in your daily practice? Has it been followed up? Did you contribute to the session in any way? When training is 'delivered' in a lecture-style format then, just like pupils in the classroom, teachers in the audience gradually switch off. Those who are more experienced teachers inevitably think 'here we go again' as some re-invention of the wheel is relayed to them. The new, keen and eager teachers are busy taking notes but invariably, when the reality of the busy working life of a teacher hits, their best intentions go out the window as they are absorbed with the day-to-day. Then there is always one antagonist in the audience. The teacher who says 'it'll never work' or 'when are we going to find the time for this'.

A much more powerful approach to introducing new techniques to teaching staff is to apply the techniques for an active learning environment. Involve teachers in the process. Let them experience the technique you are introducing and, most importantly, to give their input and feedback. After all, they are the ones who are going to be implementing any teaching strategy on a daily basis so, if they aren't fully behind the process or able to understand its purpose then, to put it bluntly, 'they won't bother'. Once you have done a brief introduction then the very best ways to experience new teaching and learning strategies is to run small 20-minute sessions where teachers go on a carousel and experience different differentiation strategies (demonstrate these across a selection of subjects – ask those teachers who are confident to deliver the individual sessions). This can be using different roles within a group. It could be that you use role play and then guide differentiated pathways or that you demonstrate questioning techniques. It may be that you look at different resources for learning that access different learning preferences, or that the SENCO runs a session based on resources for different educational needs (there are some excellent resources out there that allow staff to experience things from a pupil with a specific educational need's perspective and the SEN department will have access to these). These types of sessions give staff a flavour of different techniques – they experience the process. When you pull the body of staff back together it is important that the session remains active – it may be that staff now work in small groups of four and you give them different resources to compare, focusing on what makes a particular scenario a good approach to differentiation and what makes another bad (a comparative exercise). It might be that you ask different groups of staff to discuss the key aspects of a lesson they experienced on the carousel – positives and potential pitfalls. It is important not to group staff by subject – it is the sharing of ideas that moves learning forward at this stage. Later you might want to end the session with staff in departments where they work together to develop a lesson that demonstrates best practice in differentiation. Of course with all of this there has to be the link with differentiation and assessment for learning and so it is essential that this is discussed in the training session. What is important is that this is then briefly presented to the body of staff – this opens the floor for discussion and it is the quality of that discussion that will allow you to measure whether staff are engaged with the process. What is important following the training session is that the impetus remains. As part of your weekly bulletin ask different members of staff to contribute an idea for differentiation each week – what have they tried? Did it work? How might they adapt it in the future? Was it something that was simple to prepare? Alternatively, use your morning staff briefings to share ideas (any administrative notices can simply be emailed to staff – use the time you have collectively to focus on teaching and learning). Maintaining a focus on any strategies that we deliver on INSET days or otherwise is essential if we are to improve teaching and learning and prevent policies becoming nothing more than words on paper.

Quality assurance

I emphasise again that differentiation is not an isolated practice. It is, however, important to monitor how staff are employing differentiation strategies in the classroom to support all pupils, that best practice is shared among staff and that any poor practice is addressed. We operate in a field of high accountability and it is essential that we quality assure any process and, as part of this, formulate an action plan for taking the next logical steps to enhance a programme. The action plan needs to set clear targets or action points, success criteria (how to meet and evidence these) and a timeline for monitoring and review. If the monitoring or review process is one year down the line then the QA will have little impact and is probably not worth doing in the first place – so ensure that monitoring happens on a regular basis and that you think carefully about who will be doing this. It might be a senior leader, it might be a middle leader or it might be a teacher leader (distributing leadership is a key aspect of the self-improving system). Whoever completes the monitoring must be competent and confident – it is important that they are fully trained (perhaps through shadowing of a senior leader who is responsible for quality assurance). The monitoring process should include regular line management, team or peer meetings where performance and support for future development are discussed. It is important to remember that it is not only failing departments or teachers that should be given an action plan but outstanding departments and individuals as well – a continual drive for improvement. We must challenge and have high expectations of all and if we don't also challenge our outstanding departments or practitioners then we lead to 'coasting schools' that can quickly lose their edge.

Where a member of staff is deemed to be inadequate our first steps should be to ask why. Is it a training issue or an issue of another nature? Once we have established the root cause, we can put mechanisms in place to support that member of staff and to help them improve their practice. There must of course be a structured programme and this will focus on specific areas for improvement and success criteria. It would typically involve observations, peer observations, joint lesson planning, regularly scheduled update meetings, perhaps lesson video analysis and involve active participation. Our primary goal is to help staff to improve but, ultimately, if we have done everything we can to support that process and the member of staff is still deemed inadequate then it will be necessary to initiate competency proceedings (your HR department will provide the very best advice here). Our responsibility is both to staff and pupils in the classroom. We have a duty to ensure that our pupils are receiving the best possible education but also that we provide high quality staff training to support teachers in the classroom. Other strategies to develop staff include using professional triads where staff work as a three to develop different aspects of teaching and learning but, again, time must be invested in discussion and observations otherwise the activities are of little value. It is the focus on supporting staff to improve and not on competency that shifts the focus of observation from threat to support, thus changing the mind set of staff, resulting in more staff actively participating in and engaging with the process.

With any quality assurance process it is important that staff understand what that process is and that you communicate its purpose. The process should be timetabled and any report should be written promptly, be informative and include the specific action plan (department or individual, or both). The process may include lesson observations (these may be joint with the head of department), book samples, teacher interviews, pupil interviews and a curriculum/resource review. The purpose of any quality assurance process is to support teachers and build expertise and capacity in the education system to deliver positive outcomes for pupils. It helps to raise standards, build expectations and improve levels of consistency across schools and teaching staff. If teachers continue to repeat the same lessons year after year then they lose their current edge and they are not personalised to the pupils in their classroom. Unfortunately this does happen and it is our responsibility to keep teaching and learning at the forefront of our schools. The very best practitioners remain so because they challenge themselves and evaluate their practice, adapting to the needs of the learners in their classroom. This produces the best results. Rigorous and robust quality assurance gives confidence in teachers' judgements and provides assurance to parents and others that all pupils receive appropriate recognition for their achievements in line with agreed national standards and are progressing in line with expectations. The quality assurance process runs throughout the heart of any school and should challenge staff in a supportive and self-improving system.

Lesson study

There is an initiative, which is outlined in detail in www.lessonstudy.co.uk, that talks about slowing down the observation or learning process by focusing only on three students during the lesson observation (this technique is used very successfully in Japan). Small groups of teachers work together to develop a lesson, which one member then delivers. The focus is shifted from 'teacher delivery' to the impact on pupils (their learning and progress). The teachers select three pupils and the observation focuses on their development during the lesson. This makes the observation much more specific than if we attempt to observe both the quality of teaching and the impact on all 30 pupils (in this way it becomes too general and we may miss essential points). The three pupils (or multiples of three) are selected to reflect learners in the class, typically a low, middle and high achiever. The focus can then be on how their learning develops during the lesson – how does differentiation support progress? Do the three pupils follow different learning pathways? Do they all achieve the learning outcome? Is this at different depths? Are they involved in shaping their learning journey? How is pupil choice promoted? What resources are used? Are these pupils involved in group work? How is progress assessed? There are many more questions but you can see that by only focusing on a small number of pupils (three) we are much more likely to be able to target these questions and, most importantly, evidence them. As with any training initiative, the cost impact here is on teacher time and staffing. It is, however, an investment that is worthwhile. This type of strategy shifts the focus very much to learning and leads us in a collaborative way to look at how to improve teaching and how to improve learning, focusing on moving forwards, building on teaching strategies and focusing on development rather than on looking back and focusing too much on what didn't work. It is interesting to run a parallel observation of the lesson (by someone else) using your whole school lesson observation proforma and to see how the outcomes of the two observations compare – which is more powerful? Our ultimate goal is to develop the very best learners and the way to do this is to shift our focus to learning and work collaboratively as a group of professionals.

Summary

Embedding any policy takes time. Simply because you produce a wonderful document does not mean that staff will read it and use it. The very best schools use their training wisely and they invest in their staff. They ensure that INSET days are focused and that they develop active training strategies in which staff are involved and where their feedback is considered and used to adapt any policy (staff buy-in). They create dynamic rather than static policies. We must be very careful, however, not to over-produce policies, that is, a policy for the sake of a policy. It is important that staff are able to make connections between different strategies and that any policy is usable, manageable and effective. There are so many changes in education that we have to be cautious that we don't leave schools in a state of flux – where they are waiting for someone else to lead the way (and therefore treading water in the meantime). Teachers are often very cynical about new initiatives in education and this is mainly because many have seen them come and seen them go, only to be reinvented five years down the line under a new name. We also have to encourage teachers to 'have a go'. Many are afraid of failure. It is, however, only through something going wrong (perhaps an attempt at differentiation in your classroom didn't work as you had hoped) that we learn. We must evaluate our practice. Never be afraid to ask for support. Remember that the teaching profession is essential to bettering our economy – we have a great responsibility for the future of our nation.

The following acts as a brief checklist:

- Do all staff understand what differentiation is?
- Do they understand differentiation in the context of the school, department and classroom?
- Are they aware of school differentiation policies?
- Were staff involved in shaping this policy?
- Is this policy current and workable?
- Have staff received training in differentiation strategies?
- Was this training active?
- Are staff able to observe best practice?

- Do they have the opportunity to work with colleagues to improve their practice?
- How do staff work together?
- Do observations focus on learning?
- Does the QA process support improvement?

Conclusion

Differentiation is at the heart of personalised learning. The strategies we use aim to ensure that all pupils make the very best progress. There are many different types of differentiation including differentiation by: task, outcome, resource, pace, questioning, support, dialogue, grouping, role and assessment. Typically these strategies are used in combination and pupils are involved in shaping their own learning pathways. Our role is to facilitate and guide learning – ensuring that we create an optimum learning environment where all pupils can access learning and succeed.

The following act as a checklist that can be used as a reference guide to ensure that differentiation supports learning in your lessons.

The start of the lesson:

- ✓ How do pupils arrive to your lesson (staggered arrival, line up outside)?
- ✓ Are you greeting pupils as they arrive?
- ✓ Have you planned a simple bell-work activity and is this something pupils can just 'get on with'?
- ✓ Is this bell work personalised or a generic task?
- ✓ Do you have clear learning outcomes stating the aspect of learning and the context?
- ✓ Do pupils know and understand the success criteria or progress markers?
- ✓ Do you have these pre-prepared for pupils to stick into their books or are they kept visible at all times and returned to at key assessment opportunities?
- ✓ Have you planned a Big Question that will allow you to assess the progress of all learners?
- ✓ Is this differentiated? If so, how?
- ✓ Have you prepared a starter activity that links to the learning and that leads to or connects with the next learning cycle?
- ✓ Can all pupils access the starter activity?
- ✓ Is the starter activity differentiated (it does not have to be) and, if so, how have you allocated pupils to different activities?
- ✓ Have you planned an appropriate assessment strategy and will this allow you and pupils to know their starting point?
- ✓ Does this data inform differentiation in the main body of the lesson? How?

✓ Have you thought of targeted questioning and are you prepared to 'bounce' these around the classroom?

✓ Do you have an awareness of any misconceptions that may arise?

✓ Can you move forwards in the lesson plan or do you need to change direction?

The main body of the lesson:

✓ Are you clear on the learning purpose of each activity?

✓ Will it support pupils in working towards the learning outcomes? How?

✓ What are the success criteria?

✓ Does the activity need to be differentiated?

✓ How will differentiation best support learning?

✓ Do you use a variety of resources to ensure all pupils experience different learning styles?

✓ Do the activities engage pupils?

✓ Are all pupils able to access the activity and do they know what is expected of them?

✓ How will you assess progress and use this to guide next steps?

✓ Are pupils involved in this process and to what extent is pupil choice observed?

✓ Have pupils experienced all four stages of the learning cycle (albeit different durations)?

✓ Have you discussed learning in the lesson with any teaching assistants?

The plenary:

✓ Can all learners access the plenary activity?

✓ Does the plenary challenge learning further?

✓ Does the plenary encourage the use of combined skills and prior learning?

✓ Have you differentiated the activity?

✓ How have you differentiated the activity?

✓ Why have you differentiated the activity?

✓ Have you returned to the Big Question and allowed sufficient time for pupils to reflect and to compare their initial and final responses?

✓ Is the Big Question differentiated and, if so, how will you assess progress?

✓ Does the Big Question determine progress towards the overarching learning outcome for the lesson or series of lessons?

✓ Have you targeted questioning and asked higher-order questions to reinforce any key concepts?

✓ Can pupils identify progress in learning?

✓ Can they identify their next steps?

✓ How do you/they know?

✓ At the very end of the lesson have you revisited the bell work?

Assessment and differentiation:

- ✓ Does prior data inform planning?
- ✓ How do we use data?
- ✓ Is learning pitched at the right level?
- ✓ How is learning assessed?
- ✓ Does formative assessment direct learning pathways during the learning process?
- ✓ Do the outcomes of the assessments support pupils' next steps?
- ✓ Do the outcomes of the assessments support pupil choice?
- ✓ Is assessment data accurate and reliable?
- ✓ Is the learning environment safe with a positive climate for learning?
- ✓ Do we celebrate success and challenge misconceptions?
- ✓ Do we have high expectations of all pupils?
- ✓ Does assessment drive progress and ensure learning is accessible to all?
- ✓ Do marking and feedback inform progress?

Questioning:

- ✓ Have you established clear learning outcomes?
- ✓ Have you thought about three key questions to develop during the lesson that link to each outcome (there may only be one learning outcome but several success criteria)?
- ✓ Have you thought about how you might scaffold these questions to support pupils in achieving the desired outcomes?
- ✓ Have you considered possible questions that might branch from these key questions?
- ✓ Are you aware of possible misconceptions that may arise?
- ✓ Are you aware of the purpose of questioning – what does answering that question achieve and how does it support pupil progress?
- ✓ Have you developed the vocabulary associated with higher-order thinking and are you using it to support all pupils?
- ✓ Have you developed concepts through questioning and avoided *telling* pupils a series of facts or how to do something (knowledge-based teaching)?
- ✓ Have you extended beyond 'whole class questioning' – developing questioning through think, pair, share or other group activities?
- ✓ Are you aware of 'who' you are asking which type of question?
- ✓ Do you ensure that all pupils are exposed to higher-order questions – have you got high expectations of all pupils?
- ✓ Do you promote a safe learning environment where mistakes are valued as part of the learning process and where pupils are confident to answer questions and to ask questions of you, themselves and their peers?

Embedding differentiation:

- ✓ Do all staff understand what differentiation is?

✓ Do they understand differentiation in the context of the school, department and classroom?
✓ Are they aware of school differentiation policies?
✓ Were staff involved in shaping this policy?
✓ Is this policy current and workable?
✓ Have staff received training in differentiation strategies?
✓ Was this training active?
✓ Are staff able to observe best practice?
✓ Do they have the opportunity to work with colleagues to improve their practice?
✓ How do staff work together?
✓ Do observations focus on learning?
✓ Does the QA process support improvement?

Bibliography

Adey, P. S., Fairbrother, R. W., Wiliam, D., Johnson, B. and Jones, C. (1999) *A Review of Research Related to Learning Styles and Strategies*. London: King's College London Centre for the Advancement of Thinking.

Anderson, L. W. and Krathwohl, D. R. (Eds) (2001) *A Taxonomy for Learning, Teaching and Assessing: A Revision of Bloom's Taxonomy of Educational Objectives: Complete Edition*. New York: Longman.

Ausubel, D. P., Novak, J. D. and Helen Hanesian, H. (1978) *Educational Psychology: A Cognitive View*. New York: Holt, Rinehart and Winston.

Bartlett, J. (2013) *Becoming an Outstanding Mathematics Teacher*. Oxford: Routledge.

Black, P., Harrison, C., Lee, C., Marshall, B. and William, D. (2003) *Assessment for Learning: Putting it into Practice*. Maidenhead: Open University Press.

Black, P. and Wiliam, D. (1998) *Inside the Black Box*. London: Kings College School of Education.

Bloom, B. S. (1969) 'Some theoretical issues relating to educational evaluation'. *Educational Evaluation: New Roles, New Means*, 68, pp. 26–50.

Bloom, B. S. and Krathwohl, D. R. (1956) *Taxonomy of Educational Objectives: The Classification of Educational Goals, by a Committee of College and University Examiners. Handbook 1: Cognitive Domain*. New York: Longman.

Butler, R. (1988) 'Enhancing and undermining intrinsic motivation: the effects of task-involving and ego-involving evaluation on interest and performance'. *British Journal of Educational Psychology*, 58, pp. 1–14.

Clarke, S. (2008) *Active Learning through Formative Assessment*. London: Hodder Education.

Claxton, G. (2002) *Building Learning Power*. Bristol: TLO Limited.

Cotton, K. (1988) *Classroom Questioning*. School Improvement Research Series, p. 6. Available online at: https://www.learner.org/workshops/socialstudies/pdf/session6/6. ClassroomQuestioning.pdf (last accessed June 2014).

Cowie, B. and Bell, B. (1999) 'A model of formative assessment in science education'. *Assessment in Education Principles, Policy and Practice*, 6(1), pp. 32–42.

Davies, B. (1997) 'Listening for differences: an evolving conception of mathematics teaching'. *Journal for Research in Mathematics Education*, 28(3), 355–376.

Hill, W. E. (1915) *Puck*, 78(2018), p. 11.

Kaufman, D. B., Felder, R. M. and Fuller, H. (1999) *Annual American Society for Engineering Education Meeting Proceedings of the 1999 Annual ASEE Meeting*, Session 1430.

Kerry, T. (1998) *Questioning and Explaining in Classrooms*. London: Hodder and Stoughton

Krathwohl, D. R. (2002) 'A revision of Bloom's Taxonomy: an overview'. *Theory into Practice*, 41(4), pp. 212–218.

Ladybird (2008) *Goldilocks and the Three Bears: Ladybird Tales*. London: Ladybird (Penguin Group).

Leahy, S., Lyon, C., Thompson, M. and Wiliam, D. (2005) 'Classroom assessment: minute by minute, day by day'. *Educational Leadership* 63(3), pp. 19–24. Available online at: http://www.ascd.org/publications/educational-leadership/nov05/vol63/num03/Classroom-Assessment@-Minute-by-Minute,-Day-by-Day.aspx (last accessed July 2014).

Levin, T. and Long, R. (1981) *Effective Instruction*. Alexandria, VA: Association for Supervision and Curriculum Development.

Miller, G. A. (1968) 'The magical number seven, plus or minus two: some limits on our capacity for processing information' in *Psychology of Communication: Seven Essays*. Harmondsworth: Penguin, pp. 21–50.

Milne, A. A. (1926) *Winnie-the-Pooh*. London: Methuen and Co.

OFSTED (2012a) *Mathematics: Made to Measure*. OFSTED, May, No.110159. Available online at: www.ofsted.gov.uk/resources/110159 (last accessed October 2012).

OFSTED (2012b) *Supplementary Subject-Specific Guidance for Mathematics*, 30th October, Ref 20100015. Available online at: http://www.ofsted.gov.uk/resources/generic-grade-descriptors-and-supplementary-subject-specific-guidance-for-inspectors-making-judgements (last accessed October 2012).

OFSTED (2014a) *School Inspection Handbook April 2014*, Ref 120101. Available online at: http://www.ofsted.gov.uk (last accessed June 2014).

OFSTED (2014b) *The Framework for School Inspection, April 2014*, Ref 120100. Available online at: http://www.ofsted.gov.uk (last accessed June 2014).

Schultz, L. (2005) *Bloom's Taxonomy*. Lynn Schultz: Old Dominion University. Available online at: http://www.odu.edu/educ/llschult/blooms_taxonomy.htm (last accessed July 2014).

Scriven, M. (1967) 'The methodology of evaluation' in R. W. Tyler, R. M. Gange, and M. Scriven (Eds) *Perspectives of Curriculum Evaluation*, Chicago: RAND, 1, pp. 38–83.

Stiggens, R. J. (2005) 'From formative assessment to assessment FOR learning: a path to success in standards-based schools'. *Phi Delta Kappan*, 87(4).

Swaffield, S. (2011) 'Getting to the heart of authentic assessment for learning'. *Assessment in Education: Principles, Policy and Practice*, 18 (4), pp. 433–449.

Webb, M. and Jones, J. (2009) 'Exploring tensions in developing assessment for learning'. *Assessment in Education: Principles, Policy and Practice*, 16(2), pp.165–184.

Wiliam, D. (2011) *Embedded Formative Assessment*. Bloomington, IN: Solution Tree Press.

Electronic resources

Assessment Reform Group (2006) *The Role of Teachers in the Assessment of Learning* www.assessment-reform-group.org (last accessed July 2014).

British Museum resources http://www.britishmuseum.org/learning/schools (last accessed May 2014).

Fischer Family Trust www.fft.org.uk (last accessed May 2014).

Forensic science resources http://www.theguardian.com/teacher-network/teacher-blog/2013/mar/27/forensic-science-csi-teaching-tips-classroom (last accessed May 2014).

Millennium Mathematics Project http://motivate.maths.org/content/MultiMediaResources (last accessed June 2014).

Nuffield Foundation http://www.nuffieldfoundation.org/assessment-reform-group (last accessed April 2014).

Personal pronoun treasure hunt http://www.bbc.co.uk/skillswise/game/en27pron-game-personal-pronouns-treasure-hunt (last accessed May 2014).

RAISE online www.raiseonline.org (last accessed May 2014).

Saxon English and modern-day English http://www.essentialnormanconquest.com/media/beowulf_modern_english_04.htm (last accessed April 2014).

Should teachers use Minecraft in our classrooms? http://www.bbc.co.uk/news/education-27936946 (last accessed 20 June 2014).

Teachers TV https://www.gov.uk/government/publications/teachers-tv (last accessed June 2014).

The multiplication challenge http://nrich.maths.org/1252 (last accessed June 2014).

The coordinate challenge http://nrich.maths.org/5038 (last accessed June 2014).

UNC Centre for Teaching and Learning, *Writing Objectives using Bloom's Taxonomy* http://teaching.uncc.edu/articles-books/best-practice-articles/goals-objectives/writing-objectives-using-blooms-taxonomy (last accessed 25 July 2014).

Websites (all accessed June 2014)

http://www.autograph-maths.com

www.bbc.co.uk

http://www.drumondpark.com (LOGO board game)

www.hasbrogames.com

http://hotpot.uvic.ca

www.lessonstudy.co.uk

https://minecraft.net

www.MyMaths.co.uk

www.nasa.gov

www.nrich.maths.org

http://www.nuffieldfoundation.org/assessment-reform-group

http://www.oxforddictionaries.com

www.schoolsworld.tv

www.teachersmedia.co.uk

www.thefutureschannel.com

Index